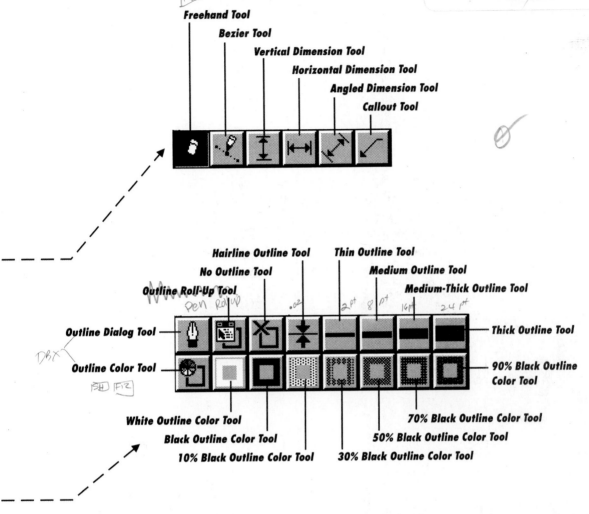

Freehand Tool [F5]

Bezier Tool

Vertical Dimension Tool

Horizontal Dimension Tool

Angled Dimension Tool

Callout Tool

Hairline Outline Tool

No Outline Tool

Outline Roll-Up Tool — Pen Rollup

Thin Outline Tool

Medium Outline Tool

Medium-Thick Outline Tool

Outline Dialog Tool

.02   2pt   8pt   16pt   24pt

Thick Outline Tool

DBX

Outline Color Tool

BH [F12]

90% Black Outline Color Tool

White Outline Color Tool

Black Outline Color Tool

10% Black Outline Color Tool

70% Black Outline Color Tool

50% Black Outline Color Tool

30% Black Outline Color Tool

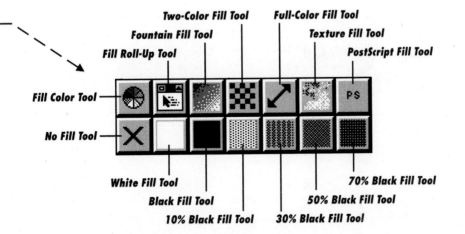

Two-Color Fill Tool

Fountain Fill Tool

Fill Roll-Up Tool

Full-Color Fill Tool

Texture Fill Tool

PostScript Fill Tool

Fill Color Tool

PS

No Fill Tool

White Fill Tool

Black Fill Tool

10% Black Fill Tool

70% Black Fill Tool

50% Black Fill Tool

30% Black Fill Tool

A Visual Approach
for the Beginner

Welcome to Quick & Easy. Designed for the true novice, this new series covers basic tasks in a simple, learn-by-doing fashion. If that sounds like old news to you, take a closer look.

Quick & Easy books are a bit like picture books. They're for people who would rather see and do than read and ponder. The books are colorful. They're full of illustrations, and accompanying text that is straightforward, concise, and easy to read.

But don't waste your time reading about our Quick & Easy books; begin learning your new software package instead. This Quick & Easy book is just the place to start.

CorelDRAW 5

Quick & Easy

CorelDRAW™ 5

Quick & Easy

Second Edition

Robin Merrin

SYBEX®

San Francisco • Paris • Düsseldorf • Soest

ACQUISITIONS EDITOR: *Savitha Varadan*
DEVELOPMENTAL EDITOR: *Steve Lipson*
EDITOR: *Michelle Nance*
TECHNICAL EDITOR: *Elizabeth Shannon*
BOOK SERIES DESIGNER: *Helen Bruno*
PRODUCTION ARTIST: *Helen Bruno*
DESKTOP PUBLISHING SPECIALISTS: *Alissa Feinberg, Deborah Maizels*
PROOFREADER/PRODUCTION ASSISTANT: *Sarah Lemas*
INDEXER: *Nancy Guenther*
COVER DESIGNER: *Archer Design*
COVER ILLUSTRATOR: *Richard Miller*

Screen reproductions produced with Collage Plus.

Collage Plus is a trademark of Inner Media Inc.

SYBEX is a registered trademark of SYBEX Inc.

TRADEMARKS: SYBEX has attempted throughout this book to distinguish proprietary trademarks from descriptive terms by following the capitalization style used by the manufacturer.

Every effort has been made to supply complete and accurate information. However, SYBEX assumes no responsibility for its use, nor for any infringement of the intellectual property rights of third parties which would result from such use.

First edition copyright ©1992 SYBEX Inc.

Library of Congress Card Number: 94-67201
ISBN: 0-7821-1461-X

Manufactured in the United States of America
10 9 8 7 6 5 4 3 2 1

To Thomas Andrew Merrin—
With love, admiration, and respect

Acknowledgments

I would like to thank my sister, Deane Swick, an accomplished graphic designer, painter, art teacher, and computer graphics instructor, for finding the time to create the original designs in CorelDRAW to be used in the lessons. The designs she created for *CorelDRAW 3 Quick & Easy* were very well received, and she was gracious enough to help us out once again.

I'm equally indebted to my husband, business partner, and technical expert, Thomas Merrin, for helping to plan and then test the lessons to make sure they worked, for suggesting improvements along the way, and for capturing every screen.

Michael Bellefeuille at Corel Corporation answered numerous questions, made sure we always had the latest software, and assisted in many ways.

Finally, I'd like to thank Savitha Varadan for asking me to write this book, Michelle Nance at SYBEX for editing it and making improvements, and Steve Lipson for assisting me throughout its development.

Contents
at a Glance

Introduction   xvi

LESSON   1
● Getting Started with
CorelDRAW   1

LESSON   2
● Getting Results with
CorelDRAW   18

LESSON   3
● Creating with Clip Art
and Symbols   34

LESSON   4
● Working with Text   49

LESSON   5
● Printing, Importing,
and Exporting Files
and Graphics   69

LESSON   6
● Maximizing Your
Results   82

LESSON   7
● Managing Files with
Corel MOSAIC   102

LESSON   8
● Tracing with CorelTRACE   118

LESSON   9
● Touching Up Photos with
Corel PHOTO-PAINT   136

APPENDIX
● Where Do I
Go from Here?   159

Index   161

Contents

Introduction   xvi

LESSON 1

Getting Started with CorelDRAW   1

Launching CorelDRAW   1
The Application Window   2
   Creating, Selecting, and Modifying Rectangles   2
   Drawing Circles and Pie Wedges   5
Saving Your Drawing   9
Changing the Outline   9
Adding and Modifying Text   11
Drawing Lines   14
Printing and Exiting   16
Finishing Touches   17

LESSON 2

Getting Results with CorelDRAW   18

Viewing What You Need   18
Starting a New Drawing   19
Drawing with the Freehand and Bezier Tools   20
Maximizing Your Effort   24
   Working with Groups of Objects   25
Rounding Rectangles   28
Zooming in for Accuracy   29
Finishing Touches   32

LESSON 3

Creating with Clip Art and Symbols 34

Using Fills and Blends 34
Importing Clip Art 36
Viewing Thumbnails with Corel MOSAIC 38
Adding Symbols 39
Arranging Objects 41
Adding Text 44
Creating a Background 45
Changing an Outline 45
Rotating Text 46
Finishing Touches 47

LESSON 4

Working with Text 49

Creating a Background 49
Curving Text 50
Placing Text on an Ellipse 50
Placing Text on a Line 53
Changing Fonts and Styles 55
Editing Text 56
Including Paragraph Text 61
Modifying Paragraph Text 63
Entering Paragraph Text 64
Modifying Several Items 65
Finishing Touches 67

LESSON 5

Printing, Importing, and Exporting Files and Graphics 69

Using Print Options 69

Printing to a File   71
Exporting a File from Corel   72
Exporting a File for Corel PHOTO-PAINT   74
Using a Template   75
   Modifying a Template   76
Copying with the Clipboard   77
Importing a File   80
Finishing Touches   81

L E S S O N   **6**

Maximizing Your Results   82

Using the Ribbon Bar   82
Setting Up the Page and Window   83
Changing Outline and Fill Defaults   84
Using Guidelines   86
   Adding Symbols and Clip Art   87
   Positioning with a Guideline   90
   Moving a Guideline   91
   Removing a Guideline   92
Changing the View   93
Adding and Modifying Text   94
   Placing Text on a Path   94
Copying Attributes   96
Using the Grid   98
Finishing Touches   99

L E S S O N   **7**

Managing Files with Corel MOSAIC   102

Getting Started   102
Working with Thumbnails in Corel MOSAIC   103
Creating a Catalog   107

Adding Keywords 109

Using Keywords to Find Files 112

Printing Thumbnails 114

    Setting Print Preferences 115

Finishing Touches 117

LESSON 8

Tracing with CorelTRACE 118

Getting Started 118

Tracing an Image 119

    Saving a Traced Image 122

Modifying a Traced Image 122

    Importing a Traced Image into CorelDRAW 122

    Modifying a Traced Image with CorelDRAW 124

    Printing a Traced Image 125

    Editing a Traced Image in Corel PHOTO-PAINT 126

More Tracing Techniques 127

    Tracing Part of an Image 127

    Tracing Several Parts of an Image 128

    Tracing Multiple Images 131

Setting Tracing Options 133

Finishing Touches 135

LESSON 9

Touching Up Photos with Corel PHOTO-PAINT 136

Getting Started 136

Opening an Image 137

Matching and Modifying Colors 138

    Zooming In 140

Enhancing Detail 141

Spraying Colors   142

Blending Colors   143

Retouching with Tools   144

Lightening an Image   145

Sharpening an Image   145

Improving Brightness and Contrast   146

Copying and Pasting   147

Blending Objects   149

Undoing Mistakes   150

Creating Objects   151

Adding Text   154

Painting Lines   155

Saving Your Image   156

Printing Your Image   156

Finishing Touches   157

APPENDIX

Where Do I Go from Here?   **159**

Index   **161**

Introduction

If you'd like someone to teach you CorelDRAW, then this book is for you. The Corel Graphics applications offer such an enormous number of features and capabilities that you might wonder where to begin. You'll find the answer here.

In nine easy lessons, you'll learn to use not only CorelDRAW, but also several other applications that are included in the suite: Corel MOSAIC, Corel-TRACE, and Corel PHOTO-PAINT. You'll also find out how to import and modify clip art images, symbols, and fonts to create professional-looking designs, drawings, and charts right away—even if you aren't a graphic designer.

This book is designed as a tutorial, which means you'll *learn by doing*. You'll draw freehand and with drawing tools. You'll create interesting effects with CorelDRAW's text-handling capabilities and trace images with Corel-TRACE. You'll enhance a photograph or other image with Corel PHOTO-PAINT tools that provide different capabilities from those in CorelDRAW. And you'll use Corel MOSAIC to help you keep your work organized and easy to locate.

The lessons themselves have two basic elements: *procedural steps* and *visual references*. The procedural steps are numbered computer operations—you'll read each step and then perform it using the mouse or keyboard. A color image accompanies many of the steps. This is your visual reference—a picture of what your screen might look like as you perform this step.

NOTE

Don't be concerned if the images you create don't match those in the book—remember, drawing is an art, not a science. The figures in the book are provided to show you an example of what the tools you'll use and drawings you'll create look like. Feel free to add elements to spice up your own drawings—one of the best ways to learn CorelDRAW is to experiment with all of the options it provides you.

ion

Hardware and Software Requirements

If you are considering the purchase of CorelDRAW, make sure your equipment meets these requirements. You must have all of these things to run CorelDRAW:

- A PC or 100%-compatible computer with either a 386DX or 486 CPU. A 486 is recommended.

- At least 8 Mb of RAM (16 Mb recommended)

- Windows 3.1

- A VGA color monitor or better (for example, a Super VGA monitor)

- A mouse or pressure-sensitive pen

- CD-ROM drive (recommended)

- Math coprocessor (recommended)

You'll probably find it is worthwhile to invest in any of the hardware and software from above that you don't have so you can get the most out of CorelDRAW.

How This Book Is Organized

The first six lessons of the book are devoted almost entirely to the drawing application CorelDRAW. It remains the most important component of the Corel package, and is probably the reason you bought the product. No matter how little computer experience or graphic design knowledge you have, you can become reasonably adept at using CorelDRAW with just a few lessons. You'll become skilled at creating drawings and business documents with original art, clip art, and CorelDRAW symbols. You'll also learn how to use your art in other documents such as brochures and newsletters.

In the last three lessons, you'll discover how to use several other major applications that are included in the package. You'll practice tracing scanned and bitmap images with CorelTRACE, and then opening them in CorelDRAW or Corel PHOTO-PAINT to make modifications. You'll use the file manager Corel MOSAIC to open, browse through, and organize files. This saves time when you're looking for a file or a clip art image. Finally, you'll have an opportunity to enhance and touch up a photograph or other image with Corel PHOTO-PAINT.

You do not have to proceed through all the lessons in order. Once you've installed CorelDRAW, we suggest you proceed through Lessons 1, 2, and 3 to give you a solid foundation in using the tools. Then, you can select the lessons that help you complete any pressing tasks. Later, you can return to other lessons, as time permits.

30 MINUTES

Getting Started with CorelDRAW

In this lesson, you'll get started creating and modifying objects and text, and begin to use the tools which are readily available in the CorelDRAW window. You'll also have a chance to work with some additional tools and something unique to CorelDRAW—roll-up windows. When you've created your first drawing, you'll also save and print it.

Launching CorelDRAW

The Corel5 group window contains the program icons that let you start the Corel applications. The applications you'll see in this window depend on the applications you installed.

The best way to become familiar with everything is to begin drawing. In this lesson, you'll create a simple design that can be used for a brochure, opening slide, or report cover. You'll use shapes, lines, text, and color.

1 If the Corel5 group window is not open, double-click the Corel5 icon at the bottom of the Program Manager window.

2 To start CorelDRAW, double-click the CorelDRAW icon in the Corel5 group window.

✱ You'll see the CorelDRAW Application window.

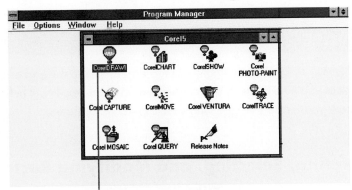

Double-click here to start CorelDRAW

The Application Window

The application window contains tools on the left that let you create and modify shapes, text, your workspace, and more. Many additional capabilities can be accessed from the menus. You have an empty drawing page on which to work, and you can begin to work with color by selecting a color from the palette shown at the bottom of the window.

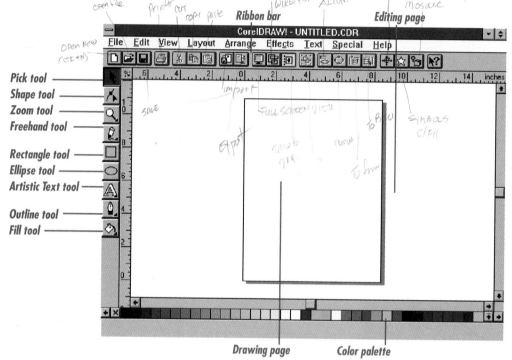

Drawing page   *Color palette*

NOTE

Before you begin, you might want to skip ahead to the end of the lesson to see what you'll be creating during the next few minutes. It will help you understand how you create a design with CorelDRAW, step by step.

Creating, Selecting, and Modifying Rectangles

1 Click the Rectangle tool.

✳ The mouse cursor is displayed as crosshairs.

2

2 Position the crosshairs in the upper-left corner of the drawing page, press the left mouse button, and drag the rectangle to the bottom right of the page. Release the mouse button when the rectangle is the size you want.

✱ Notice that you've created a rectangle on the entire page.

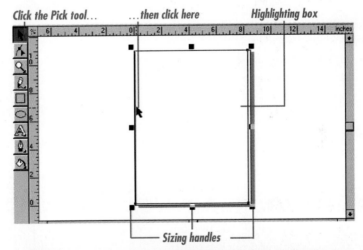

Click the Rectangle tool   Crosshairs

Place the crosshairs here   Drag the crosshairs here

3 Click the **Pick** tool at the top of the Toolbox to select the rectangle.

✱ The Pick tool is depressed and the mouse pointer changes to an arrow. When the rectangle is selected, it is surrounded by a highlighting box with eight *sizing handles.*

Click the Pick tool...   ...then click here   Highlighting box

Sizing handles

4 Now that the rectangle is selected, open the **Edit** menu and choose **Duplicate**.

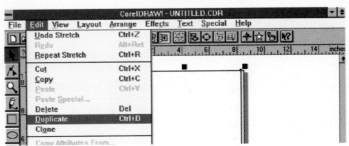

✳ A second rectangle is pasted on the page, slightly higher, and to the right of the first. It is already selected (surrounded by a highlighting box with sizing handles).

5 Point to any of the sizing handles, then drag the highlighting box in to make the rectangle smaller. (The side handles size the box horizontally; top and bottom handles size it vertically; and corner handles size the box equally in both directions.)

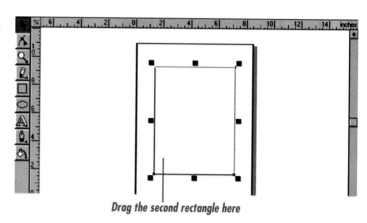

Drag the second rectangle here

6 Position the mouse pointer within the new rectangle, hold the left mouse button, and drag the rectangle to the center of the page.

✳ You now have a page with two rectangles. The inside rectangle is still selected.

Click in the color palette to fill the rectangle with a color

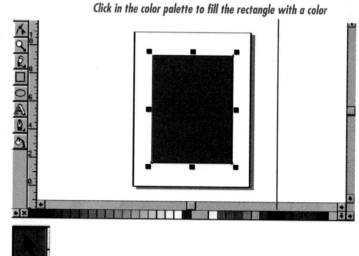

7 Move the mouse pointer to the color palette at the bottom of the screen and click a color. For our example, we'll choose the color Navy Blue.

✳ Notice the Pick tool is still depressed, so you can select the other rectangle with it.

8 Click on the outline of the larger rectangle to select it.

9 Move the mouse pointer back to the color palette at the bottom of the screen and click a color. For our example, we'll choose Blue.

✳ If you aren't happy with your selection, open the Edit menu and choose Undo Fill. Then click another color.

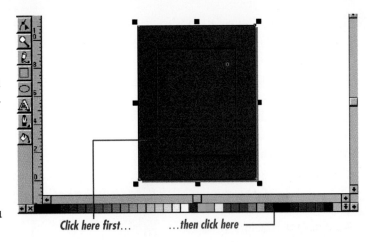

Click here first...   ...then click here

NOTE

Undo always shows your last reversible action. Use it any time you need to try something again as you progress through the lesson.

UNDO
CTL-Z

Drawing Circles and Pie Wedges

Let's make some circles and see how easily they can be modified.

NOTE

The Ctrl key enhances functionality: holding down Ctrl while you use the Ellipse tool causes Corel to create a circle instead of an ellipse. Holding down Ctrl while you use the Rectangle tool causes Corel to create a square instead of a rectangle.

CTL = Square Circle

Click the Ellipse tool

1 Point to the **Ellipse** tool and click the left mouse button.

✳ The mouse cursor changes to crosshairs again.

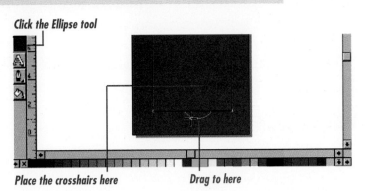

Place the crosshairs here   Drag to here

5

2 While holding down Ctrl, position the cursor near the center of the page, press the left mouse button, and drag the ellipse until you make a circle about the size you see in the illustration. When you are satisfied with the circle's size, release Ctrl and the mouse button.

3 Click the Pick tool at the top of the Toolbox to select the circle.

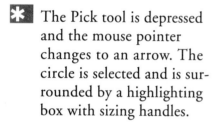

✳ The Pick tool is depressed and the mouse pointer changes to an arrow. The circle is selected and is surrounded by a highlighting box with sizing handles.

4 Move the mouse pointer back to the color palette at the bottom of the screen and click a color of your choice. We'll fill our circle with Orange.

5 Position the mouse pointer within the circle, hold the left mouse button, and drag the circle to the bottom of the smaller rectangle.

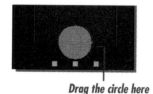

Drag the circle here

Let's turn the circle into a half-circle and fill it with a different color. In CorelDRAW, a half-circle or part of a circle is a called a *pie wedge*.

1 Click the Shape tool just below the Pick tool.

✳ The pointer changes shape to a large wedge. A *node* appears at the top or bottom of the circle. Nodes are points on lines, curves, objects, and text that give you additional control over modifications by letting you modify one part at a time.

2 Drag the node around the perimeter of the circle until only half a circle remains, then release the mouse button.

3 Click the **Pick** tool.

4 Click inside the half-circle.

✳ You'll see eight small lines with arrows on each end. This is called a *rotating and skewing highlighting box.* You can always display this box by clicking on an already selected object.

5 Point to one of the corner arrows until the cursor is displayed as crosshairs. Then drag the highlighting box around in a circle. When the box is rotated as shown in the illustration, release the mouse button.

Click the Shape tool

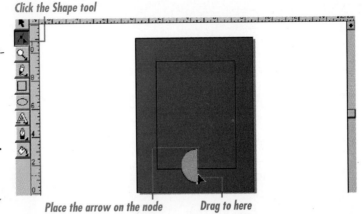

Place the arrow on the node   *Drag to here*

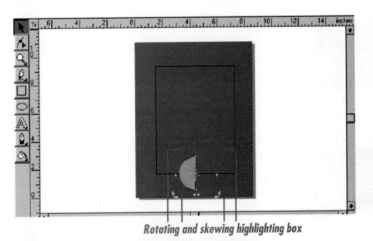

Rotating and skewing highlighting box

Drag from here...   *...to here*

NOTE

You can rotate any object using the highlighting box. Just click a selected object to display it, and drag the corner of the box.

6 Press ↑, ↓, ←, or → to make slight adjustments in the position of the half-circle.

Next, we'll create a quarter-circle, or pie wedge, of a different size using a similar set of steps.

1 Point to the **Ellipse** tool and click the left mouse button.

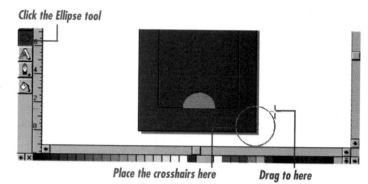

Click the Ellipse tool

2 Hold down Ctrl, position the cursor near the bottom right of the page, press the left mouse button, and drag the ellipse until you make a circle about the size you see in the illustration. When you are satisfied with the circle's size, release Ctrl and the mouse button.

Place the crosshairs here   *Drag to here*

3 Click the **Pick** tool at the top of the Toolbox to select the circle.

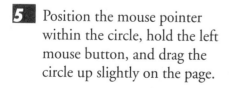

4 Move the mouse pointer back to the color palette at the bottom of the screen, press → to reveal additional colors, and click on a color of your choice. We'll fill our circle with Hot Pink.

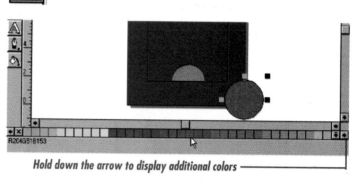

R204G518153

Hold down the arrow to display additional colors

5 Position the mouse pointer within the circle, hold the left mouse button, and drag the circle up slightly on the page.

6 Click the **Shape** tool.

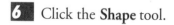

7 Drag the node around the perimeter of the circle until only a quarter-circle remains, then release the mouse button.

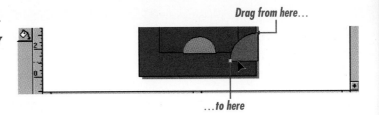

Drag from here…

…to here

＊ This quarter-circle does not have to be rotated; it is already in position.

Saving Your Drawing

Before you go any further, save your drawing.

1 Open the File menu and choose Save.

＊ The Save Drawing dialog box is displayed.

2 Move the mouse until the text cursor is in front of *.cdr and click, then press Del to delete the *.

3 Type lesson1 and click OK.

＊ The drawing is saved as *lesson1.cdr* in the directory shown under Directories.

Changing the Outline

While you are drawing, you may want to modify the color or thickness of the outlines of objects and text. For example, if you selected the color blue for the rectangle you just created, you may in fact have a blue rectangle outlined in black. To change the outline, use the Outline tool. Let's begin by removing the outline from the large rectangle.

1 Click the **Pick** tool.

2 Click near the border of the large rectangle to select it.

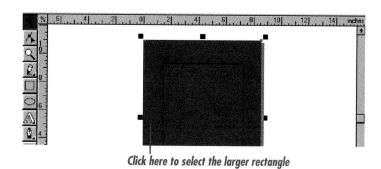

Click here to select the larger rectangle

3 Click the **Outline** tool (on the arrow).

✱ The Outline menu is opened. In CorelDRAW, the menus that open from the Toolbox are called *flyout* menus.

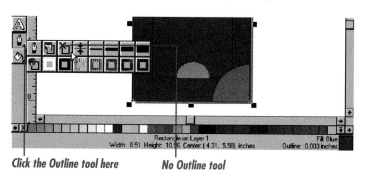

Click the Outline tool here   *No Outline tool*

4 Click the **No Outline** tool.

✱ The outline is removed.

NOTE

Use this technique to remove the outline from any object on a page. Remember to use the Pick tool to select it first before you open the Outline flyout menu.

Now change the outline color of the smaller rectangle.

1 Click the **Pick** tool, if necessary.

2 Click near the border of the small rectangle to select it.

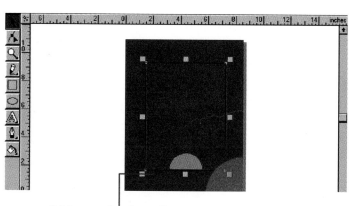

Click here to select the smaller rectangle

3 Click and hold the **Outline** tool.

4 Click the **Outline Dialog** tool from the flyout.

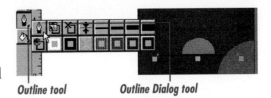

Outline tool   *Outline Dialog tool*

✳ The Outline Pen dialog box is displayed.

5 Click the **Color** button (shown to the right of *Color*).

6 Click a color of your choice.

7 Click **OK** to close the dialog box.

Click the Color button...   *...then click a color here*

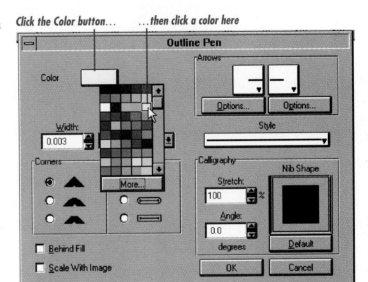

Adding and Modifying Text

With a basic background design in place, let's add text to the page.

1 Click the **Artistic Text** tool.

✳ If the Artistic Text tool is not shown, hold the mouse button down while you point to the Paragraph tool arrow to open the menu, then click the *A* icon.

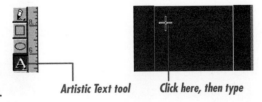

Artistic Text tool   *Click here, then type*

2 Click in the upper-left corner of the smaller rectangle to add text to it.

3 Type the words WELCOME TO CorelDRAW 5, pressing ↵ after each of the three words.

Type the text here

4 Click the Pick tool to select the text you just typed.

* Now you can modify the text.

5 Point to any of the sizing handles, then drag the highlighting box out to make the text larger. This increases the point size, and CorelDRAW also maintains the proportions of the letters.

Drag out from here

* Use this technique to size the text as you want it.

6 While the text is still selected, click a color in the color palette.

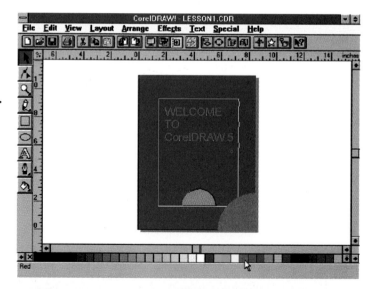

7 Open the Text menu and choose Text Roll-Up.

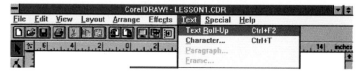

✱ This is the first roll-up window you've used. A roll-up is similar in purpose to a dialog box, but you can position it anywhere in the editing window for quick access, and "roll it up" when you don't need it so it takes up very little space.

8 Click the **Center Justification** button, then click **Apply**.

✱ The text is centered in its selection box. You may have to drag the selection box to the center of the page.

Click the Center Justification button...   *...then click Apply*

Add additional text below, following the same steps.

1 Click the **Artistic Text** tool again.

2 Click near the center of the smaller rectangle to add text to it.

3 Type the words **The Revolution Continues**..., pressing ↵ after each of the three words.

4 Click the **Pick** tool to select the text you just typed.

Drag the handles out

5 Point to any of the sizing handles, then drag the highlighting box to make the text larger.

6 While the text is still selected, click a color in the
color palette.

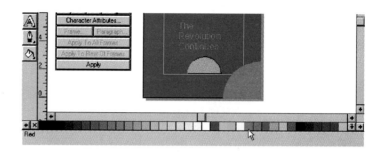

7 In the Text roll-up, click the
Center Justification button,
then click **Apply**.

* The text **The Revolution
Continues…** is centered
in its selection box. You may
have to drag the selection box
to the center of the page.

8 Click the **Minimize** button to
"roll up" the Text roll-up.

Center Justification button   *Click the Minimize button*

Drawing Lines

Let's add a line above the word *WELCOME* to make the drawing more
interesting.

1 Click the Freehand tool.

Freehand tool   *Freehand tool*

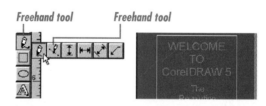

NOTE

When using the Zoom, Freehand, and Text tools, you'll need to hold the mouse button down for an extra second on the arrow to open the flyout menu. Just clicking
will simply select the tool that's currently shown.

✱ The cursor is displayed as crosshairs.

Click here...   ...then click here

2 Click the left mouse button on the line's starting point, then press and hold Ctrl while you click the ending point.

NOTE

When you hold down Ctrl, CorelDRAW draws a straight line from the starting point you indicate to the ending point. If you want to draw a line that is not straight (for example, to draw a curve or shape), use this tool and drag the mouse without pressing Ctrl.

3 Take a minute to experiment with the **Freehand** tool. Click at a starting point somewhere on the side of the page, and make some wavy lines.

Try using the Freehand tool to add lines

Let's add a broken line to the lower-right corner of the page.

1 Click the **Freehand** tool.

2 Click with the left mouse button on the starting point for the line, then press and hold down Ctrl while you click the ending point.

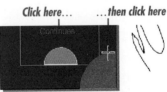

Click here...   ...then click here

3 Click the **Outline** tool, then click the **Outline Dialog** tool.

✱ The **Outline Pen** dialog box is opened.

Outline tool   Outline Dialog tool

4 In the **Outline Pen** dialog box, type **0.100** in the **Width** box to make the line thicker.

5 Click the **Style** box to display the different available line styles.

6 Click on the broken line to select it. This will make the line you've already drawn into a broken line.

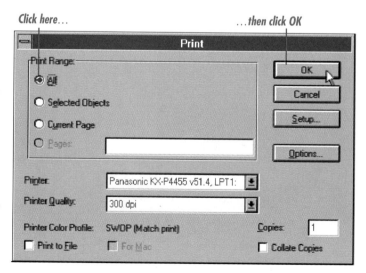

Change the width... ...click here... ...then select a style

7 Click **OK**.

Printing and Exiting

Let's finish this lesson by saving, printing, and exiting.

1 Because you've changed your drawing since you last saved it, open the **File** menu and choose **Save**. The Save Drawing dialog box won't be displayed. CorelDRAW will simply save this drawing with the name you already gave it, *lesson1.cdr*.

2 Open the **File** menu and choose **Print**.

✳ The Print dialog box is displayed. The options displayed depend on the printer you have installed under Windows.

3 To print the entire drawing page, select **All**, and click **OK**.

Once your drawing is printed, you are ready to exit CorelDRAW. Open the File menu and choose **Exit** to close CorelDRAW and return to Windows.

Finishing Touches

We added some additional straight, broken, and wavy lines at the top and bottom and changed their thickness and color. We also added some stars to the top, using CorelDRAW symbols. You'll learn how to do this in Lesson 3.

Once you've tried out your own finishing touches, be sure to save your drawing by opening the **File** menu and choosing **Save**.

LESSON

2

30 MINUTES

Getting Results with CorelDRAW

In this lesson, you'll combine some of the techniques you learned in the previous lesson with new ones, to learn how to quickly design a page that doesn't look "thrown together." As in the previous lesson, you may want to look ahead to the drawing at the end of the lesson to see where you are going.

Viewing What You Need

CorelDRAW's application window contains some items that you can turn on or off and rearrange. Among the most useful are the *rulers* and *Toolbox*. Rulers help you judge the size and position of objects you draw. You've used the Toolbox already to select drawing tools. For this lesson, we'll turn the rulers on if they aren't already, to see if you find them helpful, and display the Toolbox differently from the default location at the left side of the window.

> **NOTE**
>
> If a display item is already turned on, you'll see a check next to it on the menu. If you choose a checked item, it is turned off. However, although the Toolbox is displayed when you first install CorelDRAW, the check is shown on the cascading menu next to the Visible option.

1 To display the rulers (if they are not currently displayed), open the **View** menu and click **Rulers**.

✳ The rulers' 0,0 point is the lower-left corner of your drawing page.

2 To move the Toolbox, open the **View** menu and click **Toolbox**, then click **Floating**.

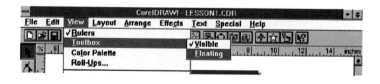

✱ CorelDRAW treats the floating Toolbox like a window,
which you can move by dragging and resize by dragging on
the window border.

3 To display all the tools in the
Toolbox, open the **Control**
menu on the Toolbox and
click **Grouped** to ungroup the
tools and remove the check.

✱ The tools are grouped by
default.

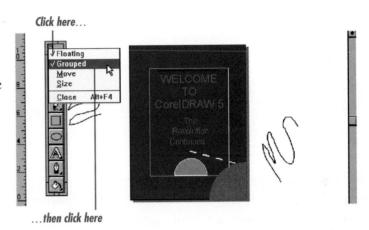

Click here...

...then click here

The status line is displayed by default at the bottom of the window. As you
choose tools and create, select, and modify objects, you'll see information
about them in this area.

Starting a New Drawing

If you still have your previous drawing open, you'll want to save it and then
start on a clean page.

1 Open the File menu and
choose New.

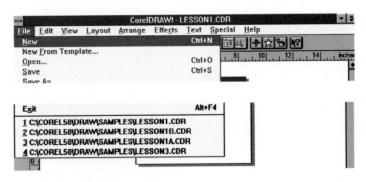

✱ You'll notice that the last four
files you worked on are listed
at the bottom of this menu.
When you want to work on
the **lesson1.cdr** file again,
click it here and CorelDRAW
will open it again.

2 If you haven't saved your drawing from the previous lesson, choose **Yes** when you are prompted.

You now have an empty page on which to draw.

Drawing with the Freehand and Bezier Tools

We'll begin this drawing by creating a color background. Then we'll draw a design with the Freehand and Bezier tools.

NOTE

The Bezier tool differs from the Freehand tool in that with the Freehand tool, you drag the mouse to draw lines, while with the Bezier tool you click the mouse at each turning point in the line and CorelDRAW connects the points.

1 Point to the **Rectangle** tool and click the left mouse button. Then draw a rectangle that covers the entire page.

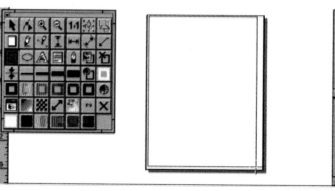

2 Click the **Pick** tool. This will select the rectangle, and a highlighting box with handles will appear.

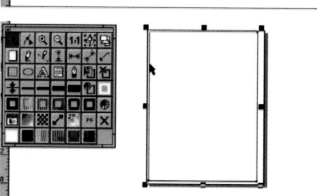

LESSON 2

3 Click the Fountain Fill tool.

Click the Fountain Fill tool

* The Fountain Fill dialog box opens.

4 Click on the arrow to open the Type list box, then click Linear.

* You are going to custom blend a color by selecting starting (From) and ending (To) colors from the color palettes. Then you'll fill the rectangle with that blend, from top to bottom.

5 Click From to open the color palette in order to select one of the colors to blend, then click a color of your choice in the color palette.

6 Click To in order to select the second color to blend, then click a color of your choice in the color palette.

7 Click OK to close the dialog box and fill the rectangle with a linear fountain fill.

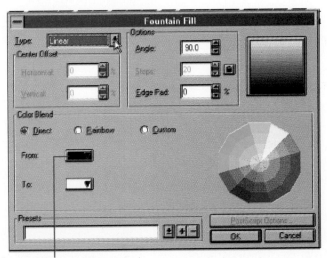

Click here, then click a color

✳ The linear fill changes the
color in one direction; in this
case, from the top to bottom
of the rectangle.

8 Follow the preceding steps to
create a second rectangle in
the bottom 25% of the page
and fill it with a fountain fill
using two different (From and
To) colors.

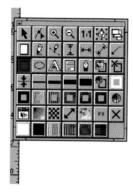

✳ You now have a background
for your design.

You'll start your design by drawing with the Bezier tool.

1 Click the Bezier tool.

Click here

Draw a leaf design

2 Off to the side of the drawing
page, draw a leaf design like
the one shown. Click the starting point and then click the
ending point of each line; the
pencil will connect each point
to the previous point when
you click. Make your last click
at the point where you started
in order to complete the object. Otherwise, CorelDRAW
will treat it as a line and you
will not be able to fill it with a
color.

Click back at starting point when finished

NOTE

If you aren't happy with your leaf design, you can open the Edit menu and choose Delete to delete the whole object, then try again. The Bezier tool is still active, so you just have to click the starting point and begin drawing again. If you are satisfied with all of the object except the last line, open the Edit menu and instead choose Undo to delete only the very last line you drew. You'll see the command Undo Curve Append.

NOTE

CorelDRAW has a feature called AutoJoin, which automatically connects two endpoints even if you do not draw them in exactly the same place. If you place the ending point within five pixels of the starting point, CorelDRAW will recognize that you meant to connect those points and do it for you.

If you aren't satisfied with your efforts, you can try drawing the leaf with the Freehand tool. The Bezier tool lets you draw the line more precisely, but this of course takes practice.

1 Click the **Pick** tool, then click the outline of your drawing to select it.

2 Press Del to delete it so you can start again.

3 Click the **Freehand** tool.

Click the Freehand tool

4 Drag the cursor on the page to create a leaf, but don't hold down Ctrl since you don't want CorelDRAW to draw straight lines.

5 Click the Shape tool.

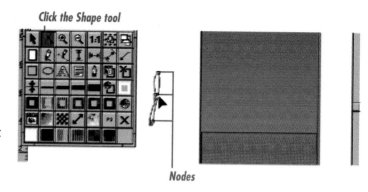

Click the Shape tool

Nodes

✱ You'll notice that nodes are displayed along the curves. (As you saw in Lesson 1, nodes are points on lines, curves, objects, and text that give you additional control over modifications by letting you modify one part at a time.)

6 Point to and drag any of the nodes if you want to modify the shape and size of the drawing.

Maximizing Your Effort

CorelDRAW allows you to make many images from one drawing.

1 Click the Pick tool, then click the outline of your drawing to select it.

2 Place the cursor in the center of the highlighting box and drag the object to the lower-left corner of your page.

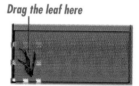

Drag the leaf here

✱ The object is still selected, so you can now duplicate it.

3 Open the Edit menu and choose Duplicate.

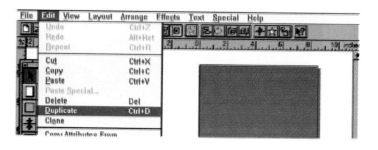

4 Choose Repeat Duplicate.

✱ Two copies of the object are pasted on the page, slightly above, and to the right of the first. The top object is selected.

5 Drag the top object to the lower-right section of the page.

Drag the top object here...

6 Click the remaining duplicate to select it, then drag it to the bottom center of the page.

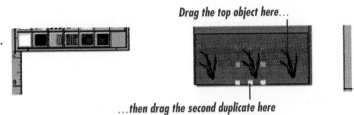

...then drag the second duplicate here

7 Hold down Shift while you click inside the first object on the left, then the second, and then the third object.

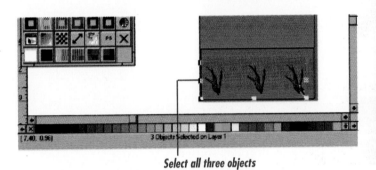

Select all three objects

This will select all three objects, so that you can apply a command to all three at the same time. You'll notice the highlighting box surrounds all three, and in the status line, it shows that three objects are selected.

Working with Groups of Objects

Now we'll apply a command to all three selected objects.

1 Open the Effects menu and choose Transform Roll-Up.

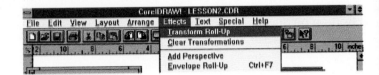

GETTING RESULTS WITH CORELDRAW

NOTE

The Transform roll-up lets you resize, scale, rotate, skew, and mirror objects and move them on the page.

2 In the Transform roll-up, click the middle button, which lets you stretch and mirror the selected image.

3 Under Scale, enter 150 for both H and V.

4 Click the Horizontal Mirror button.

5 Click Apply To Duplicate.

6 Click Apply.

✳ The new objects are at the bottom of the page and are selected.

7 Drag the selection box so that all the objects are in the bottom center of the page.

8 Double-click the Close box on the Transform roll-up to close it, or click the Minimize button to leave only the title bar visible (roll it up).

✳ Roll up or close the Transform menu, if you wish.

Click to Stretch and Mirror   *Horizontal Mirror*

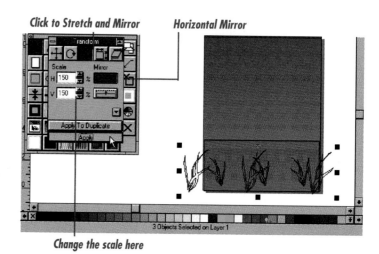

Change the scale here

Let's select the three original objects again and duplicate them, this time using slightly different techniques.

1 Click the **Pick** tool.

✱ You'll use it to draw a box around the leaves. In CorelDRAW, this box is called a *marquee selection box*.

2 Start above the upper-left corner of the group of leaves (in a blank area of the window) and drag the cursor to the lower-right corner, then release the mouse button.

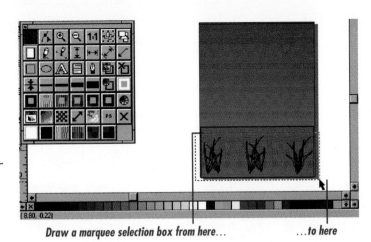

Draw a marquee selection box from here... ...to here

✱ The leaves are all selected.

3 Open the **Edit** menu and choose **Copy**.

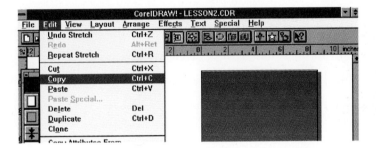

✱ A copy of the leaves is pasted to the Windows Clipboard.

4 Open the **Edit** menu and choose **Paste**.

✱ The copy is pasted to the page right on top of the original.

NOTE

The copy and paste combination is very useful for copying objects from one drawing to another.

5 Click inside one of the new, selected objects and drag all three new objects up from the originals so they are more visible in the drawing.

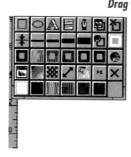

Drag the new objects from here...

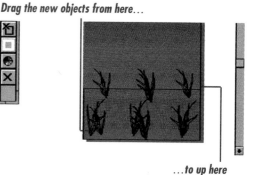

...to up here

6 Click each object and then click a color in the color palette.

* You can scroll the color palette to display more colors by holding down the mouse button on either the left or right arrow and clicking the up arrow in the lower-right corner of the window.

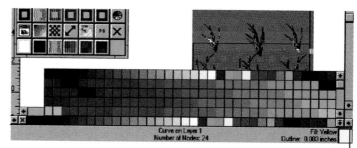

Click here to open the color palette

For additional practice, try using the Bezier and Freehand tools to draw some flowers in your garden.

NOTE

If you aren't satisfied with the results, you can use some of the symbols found in the Plants category of the fonts that come with CorelDRAW. You'll learn how to include symbols in your drawings in Lesson 3.

Rounding Rectangles

By now, you know how to draw perfect rectangles. They were covered in Lesson 1 and earlier in this lesson. Rounding the corners can sometimes make rectangles look more interesting.

1   Click the Rectangle tool.

2   Draw a rectangle on the bottom of the page, about 4 inches wide and 1 $\frac{1}{2}$ inches high. Look at the ruler and status line to help you with this.

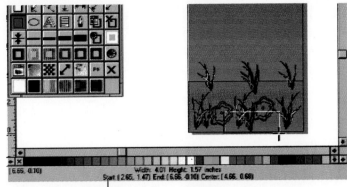

Watch the status line as you draw

3   Use the Pick tool to select the rectangle, then click a color in the palette. We selected Black to fill the rectangle.

4   Select the Shape tool.

✱   Four nodes are displayed, one on each corner.

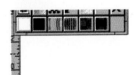
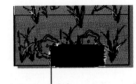

Drag any node in toward the center

5   Point to any of the nodes and drag it slightly toward the center of the rectangle.

As you drag, the rectangle's corners are rounded. Try dragging the mouse pointer in and out until you achieve the effect of slightly rounded corners.

Zooming in for Accuracy

Let's put one more rounded rectangle in the large rectangle with rounded corners and insert some text in the rectangle we just created. Since you are going to be working on only a small part of the drawing for a few minutes, you may want to increase the size of that part of the drawing temporarily. CorelDRAW has tools that change your view without changing the drawing.

1 Click the **Zoom In** tool. Zoom In is the first Zoom tool on the left, and it has a + (plus sign) in the middle of a magnifying glass.

Click the Zoom In tool

✳ The cursor changes to a magnifying glass.

2 Click at the top left of the imaginary box and drag the mouse to the bottom right of the box, then release the mouse button.

Draw a box from here...   *...to here*

✳ The area you selected is magnified.

Remember, you can move and reshape the Toolbox if it is in your way by dragging the window border in or out. You may want to move and reshape the Toolbox fairly often as you are working, especially in a zoom mode.

Let's add text to the rectangle.

1 Click the **Text** tool, then click in the rectangle to place the cursor where you want to start typing.

2 Type **Lesson 2.**

3 Click the **Pick** tool to select the text **Lesson 2.**

30

4 Point to any of the sizing handles, then hold the mouse button while you drag the highlighting box out to make the text larger.

Drag a sizing handle to make the text larger

5 With the text still selected, click a color in the color palette.

* If the text is surrounded by thick black lines, you need to change the outline or you won't see the color fill.

Select No Outline tool

Or select a thinner outline

6 Select a thinner outline from the Toolbox or click the **No Outline** tool if you don't want any outline on your text.

We're going to add a smaller rounded rectangle inside the first rectangle.

1 Use the **Rectangle** tool to draw a rectangle that's about 3 inches wide and .15 inches high at the top of the first rectangle.

2 Use the **Pick** tool to select the new rectangle, then click a color in the palette.

You can make it even larger on-screen so you can work on it more easily.

1 Click the **Zoom To Selected** tool.

Click the Zoom To Selected tool

* This magnifies the selected object, which in this case is the new rectangle.

2 Click the **Shape** tool.

3 Point to one of the nodes and drag it slightly toward the center of the rectangle.

4 To return to full page view, click the **Zoom To Page** tool.

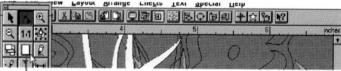

Click the Zoom To Page tool

* Zoom To Page is the last Zoom tool.

Finishing Touches

You can put some finishing touches on the drawing that will give you additional practice with tools you used in this lesson and the previous one. The final drawing shows these added features:

- Another small rectangle under the number 2.

- A pie wedge in the upper-left corner, filled with a linear fountain fill.

- The text **CorelDRAW Quick & Easy** in a different font.

- Flowers, which we found in the Symbols roll-up under Plants. You'll learn to use CorelDRAW symbols in Lesson 3 and can come back and try them on this drawing if you like.

- Multiple additional flowers in varying sizes and shapes, created using the Transform roll-up.

Try to add these elements using the steps provided in Lessons 1 and 2. And try out some ideas of your own.

We also changed the fonts for the text. You'll learn about modifying fonts in Lesson 4.

When you are finished, be sure to save your drawing using the steps in Lesson 1.

Creating with Clip Art and Symbols

30 MINUTES

Whether you are an artist or a business user, you'll find that CorelDRAW's library of clip art and symbols can help you create beautiful designs and business documents. This lesson teaches you to import clip art, select symbols, and change them to suit your needs. As before, you may want to look at our final creation at the end of the lesson before you start working.

Using Fills and Blends

First, let's create a simple background design using Fills and Blends.

1 Click the **Rectangle** tool. Then draw a rectangle that covers the upper-left quarter of the page.

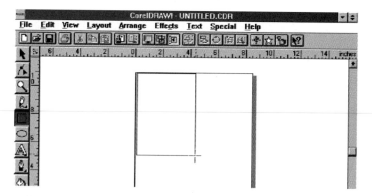

2 Use the **Rectangle** tool to draw three more rectangles, each the same size and covering a quarter of the page.

3 Draw one last rectangle in the center of the page.

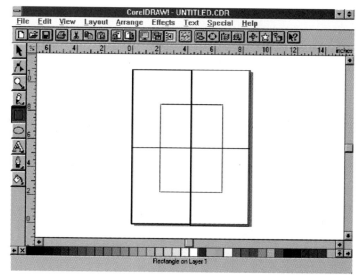

Now, fill each background rectangle with a textured fill, instead of a solid color.

1 Click the Pick tool, then click the first rectangle you drew.

✱ The rectangle is selected.

2 Open the Fill flyout and click the Texture Fill tool.

Pick tool   *Texture Fill tool*

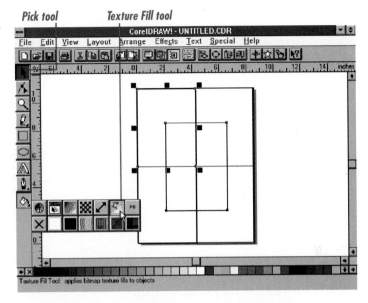

✱ The Texture Fill dialog box is displayed.

3 Choose Styles from the Texture Library drop-down list.

4 Choose a fill from the Texture List.

5 Click OK.

Click here...   *...then click here*

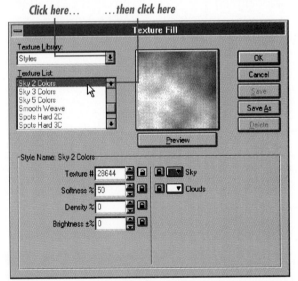

✱ You'll see the results of your selection in the first rectangle. The Pick tool is still selected.

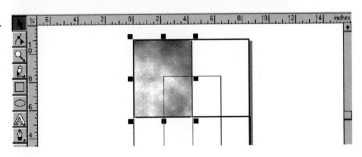

6 Follow steps 4 and 5 to fill the remaining three background rectangles.

7 Click the fifth rectangle and click a color of your choice in the color palette at the bottom of the window.

* You now have a background for your design.

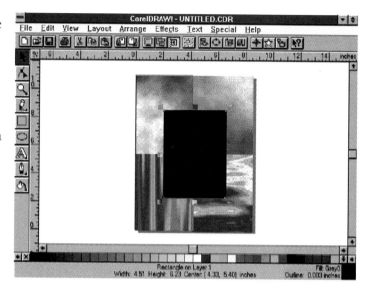

Importing Clip Art

Each piece of clip art you selected during the CorelDRAW installation is stored as a file. If you know the name of the file that you want to use, you can import the file quickly.

NOTE

The CorelDRAW package includes a book which shows you all the clip art and symbols on the CD-ROM. Some clip art is also included on the Setup disks, so it is available even if you don't have a CD-ROM drive. We'll use some of the clip art in this lesson. You can use any clip art you've installed from disk if you are not running CorelDRAW from CD-ROM.

1 Open the **File** menu and choose **Import**.

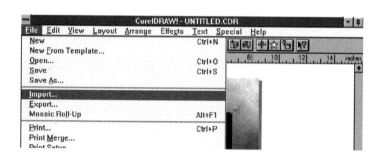

✳ The Import dialog box is displayed.

✳ If you are running CorelDRAW from CD-ROM, the clip art is on that drive. (usually D: or E:), so select that drive from the Drives drop-down list.

2 Scroll down the list box until you see the **clipart** directory, then double-click it.

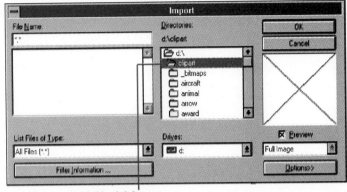

Double-click here

3 Scroll down the list box again, this time until you see the **fantasy** directory, then double-click it.

✳ You'll see a list of the files in the **clipart\fantasy** directory in the File Name box.

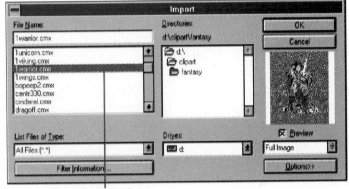

Select the clip art here

4 Scroll the box until you see **1warrior.cmx**, then click it.

✳ That's the first file you'll be importing to your drawing.

5 Click **OK**.

✳ The dialog box closes and a figure of a warrior is on your drawing page, surrounded by a highlighting box.

Drag the clip art here

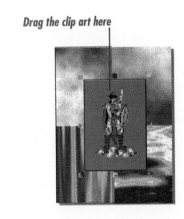

6 Drag the sizing handles to change the figure's size and proportions, or place the mouse cursor within the box and drag it in order to move it around.

NOTE

The status line shows the scale factor. Watch it to help you resize the object correctly and keep it in proportion.

That's all there is to importing clip art if you know what kind of image you are looking for.

Viewing Thumbnails with Corel MOSAIC

If you aren't sure what kind of clip art you want to include, but you have a category in mind, you can look through a group of clip art figures and select what you want from a *thumbnail*, or miniature, using Corel MOSAIC. Corel MOSAIC is a visual file manager included with CorelDRAW. You can use Corel MOSAIC to see thumbnails of all the files in a directory, and then import the pictures from there.

1 Open the File menu and choose Mosaic Roll-Up.

✱ The Mosaic roll-up is displayed.

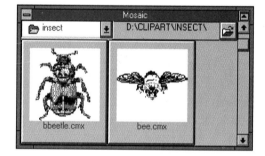

2 Double-click corel50 in the Directories drop-down list.

3 Double-click clipart in the list, then double-click insect.

✱ If you need to change the drive, click the Open button, then select another drive from the Drives drop-down list and select the directory there.

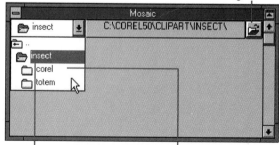

Click to change drives

Double-click here first...   *...then double-click here*

Drag the butterfly from here...   ...to here

* The Mosaic window shows thumbnails of all the files that are in the **clipart\insect\corel** directory.

4 Drag the butterfly (**butfly3-.cmx**) from the Mosaic window to the top of the page.

5 Click on the **Minimize** button in the **Mosaic** roll-up, then drag it out of your drawing area.

6 Drag any of the sizing handles to change the size and proportions of the butterfly, and drag it to the upper-left corner of the page.

Drag a sizing handle to rotate the butterfly

7 Click the butterfly to display the rotating and skewing box.

8 Drag the handles to rotate the butterfly slightly.

NOTE

There are several helpful file management tools in Corel MOSAIC to help you organize and find your own files and CorelDRAW's clip art. Lesson 7 covers many of the capabilities of Corel MOSAIC.

Adding Symbols

Some of the items in the drawing are not clip art, but instead CorelDRAW symbols. There are also thousands of symbols available to use in a variety of ways.

1 From the Special menu, choose Symbols Roll-Up.

✳ The Symbols roll-up is displayed. The drop-down list shows the categories of symbols you installed.

Press here to display more categories

2 Choose Wingdings from the drop-down list.

3 Change the size of the symbol you'll select to 2.00 inches by scrolling the Size text box.

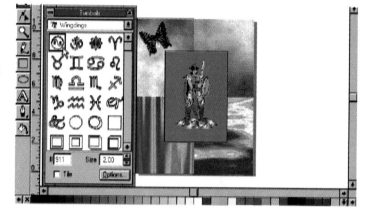

4 Drag a symbol from the roll-up to the editing window, or choose a symbol by typing its number, if you know it. We chose Wingding 911.

✳ Remember to use the scroll bar to display all the symbols in this category. Look at the bottom of the roll-up to see the symbol number.

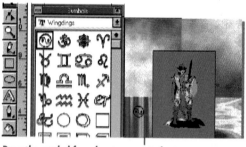

Drag the symbol from here...   ...to here

5 Click the **Minimize** button on the **Symbols** roll-up, then drag it out of your drawing area.

Arranging Objects

You can duplicate symbols, then change their outlines and add color, treating each as a group of objects instead of just one object to give you more flexibility.

1 Click the **Pick** tool at the top of the Toolbox and click the symbol to select it.

2 Move the mouse pointer to the color palette at the bottom of the screen and click a color of your choice.

* Notice that the color is applied to part of the symbol, since the symbol is now a group of parts.

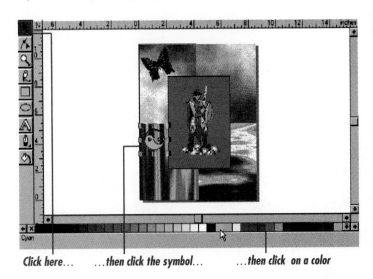

Click here...   *...then click the symbol...*   *...then click on a color*

3 With the symbol still selected, open the **Edit** menu and choose **Duplicate**.

* A copy of the symbol is pasted on the page, slightly above and to the right of the original. It is already selected.

4 Point to any of the sizing handles, then drag the highlighting box out to make the symbol larger.

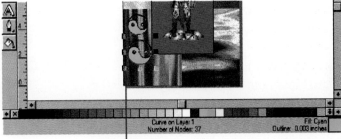

Drag out from here

5 Position the mouse pointer within the new symbol, hold the left mouse button, and drag the duplicate below the original.

The second symbol is still selected. Let's break the symbol apart into a group of objects, so you can apply several colors instead of just one.

1 Open the **Arrange** menu and choose **Break Apart**.

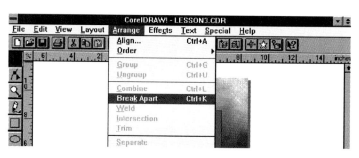

2 Open the **Edit** menu and choose **Clone**.

✱ When you use Clone to copy an object, changes that are subsequently made to the original are also applied by CorelDRAW to its clone. This is not true of Duplicate.

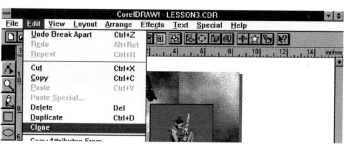

3 Point to any of the sizing handles of the new object, then drag the highlighting box in to make the symbol smaller.

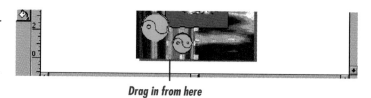

Drag in from here

4 Position the mouse pointer within the newest symbol, hold the left mouse button, and drag it below and to the right of the original.

5 Click the **Pick** tool, then click the larger symbol to select it.

Click the larger symbol

6 Click the **Zoom** tool.

7 Click the **Zoom To Selected** tool.

Click here

8 Click on the smaller left circle within the symbol to select it.

9 Move the mouse pointer back to the color palette at the bottom of the screen and click a color of your choice.

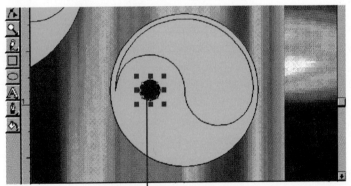

Click here, then choose a color

10 Click on the outer circle of the symbol to select it.

11 Move the mouse pointer back to the color palette at the bottom of the screen and click a color of your choice.

12 Repeat steps 10 and 11 for the tear-shaped object.

Your color selections have also been applied to the clone of the symbol.

The smaller right circle can no longer be seen. You can fix this problem with another command on the Arrange menu. The tear-shaped object is still selected.

1 Open the **Arrange** menu and choose **Order**, then choose **Back One**.

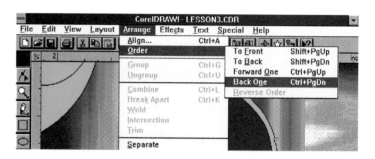

✱ If the smaller right circle is still not visible, choose the Arrange, Order command repeatedly, choosing Back One until you can see all parts of the symbol. You may want to try other options on the menu to see how the Order command works.

2 To return to full page view when you are finished, click the **Zoom** tool, then click the **Zoom To Page** tool from the **Zoom** flyout.

Click the Zoom To Page tool

✱ Notice that your cloned symbol has been filled with the same colors as the original but the Order change has not been applied.

Adding Text

The last new element in the drawing is the rotated text on the right edge of the page. First, you'll create a background for the text, and then you'll rotate it.

Creating a Background

Let's create a colorful background for our text.

1 Point to the **Rectangle** tool and click the left mouse button. Then draw a rectangle that covers the right edge of the page.

2 Move the mouse pointer to the color palette at the bottom of the screen and click a color of your choice.

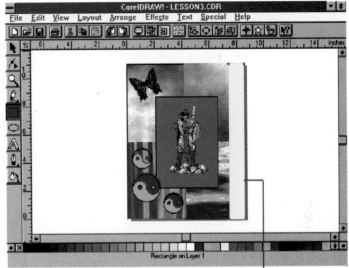

Draw a rectangle here

3 Click the **Freehand** tool.

4 Hold the mouse button down and drag the cursor on the page to create a wavy line alongside the rectangle.

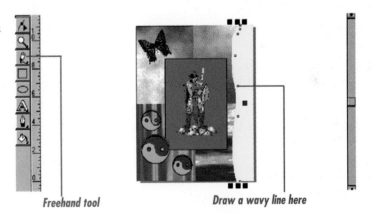

Freehand tool   *Draw a wavy line here*

Changing an Outline

In order to achieve the same effect you see shown in the illustration, you'll need to make some modifications. You'll need to change the width of the rectangle's outline, and then you'll select a color for the outline.

1 Click the Outline tool, then click the Outline Dialog tool to open the Outline Pen dialog box.

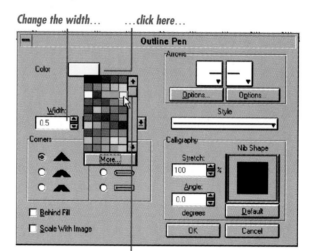

Outline Dialog tool

2 Change the Width to 0.5 inches.

Change the width...   *...click here...*

3 Click the Color button to open the palette, then click the same color you chose for the rectangle.

4 Choose OK. You may need to click the Pick tool, then drag the wavy line to the rectangle to make the two objects overlap.

...then click a color

Now you can type the text, rotate it, and place it in the rectangle.

NOTE

In this case, it may be easier to work off the page for a minute since you have several objects in the area where the text will be placed.

Rotating Text

Let's begin by rotating the text.

1 Click the Artistic Text tool.

2 Move the cursor to the right of the page and type Clip Art & Symbols.

Click here...

...then click and type here

3 Click the **Pick** tool to select the text **Clip Art & Symbols**.

4 Stretch the highlighting box until you are satisfied with the text size.

5 Click inside the text.

✱ You'll see the *rotating and skewing highlighting box*.

Rotating and skewing highlighting box

6 Point to the right corner arrow until the cursor is displayed as crosshairs. Then drag the highlighting box around in a circle. When the box is rotated 90 degrees, release the mouse button.

7 Click to select the text and drag it to the right edge of the page.

Rotate, then drag the text here

8 Move the mouse pointer to the color palette at the bottom of the screen and click a color to change the color of the text.

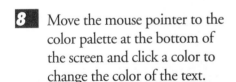

Finishing Touches

We finished our drawing by adding some shapes, clip art, and symbols, as you can see in the final illustration. Try out some ideas of your own, then be sure to save your drawing. These are the things we added:

- An ellipse with the text **Lesson 3**.

- A rectangle with the text **CorelDRAW 5**.

- A parrot, which is found in the **clipart\bird** directory, as **parrot3.cmx**.

- Two additional symbols in the bottom right: #35 in the **Landmarks** category and #70 in the **GeographicSymbols** category.

- An outline change to the rectangle in the middle.

- Different fills and blends to the background—experiment with these if you have time.

And, we changed the fonts for the text. Lesson 4 covers modifying fonts.

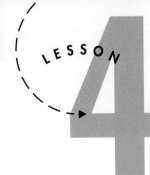

LESSON 4

Working with Text

30 MINUTES

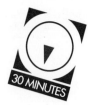

You've included text in your drawings in the last three lessons; however, you haven't had a chance to modify it, other than to change its size or color. In this lesson, we'll show you how to change the font and style and to bring in text from another application such as your word processing program. You'll also learn how to place the text on a curve.

Creating a Background

We'll begin this drawing by creating a color background. Then we'll create a design with text.

1 Click on the **Rectangle** tool with the left mouse button. Then draw a rectangle that covers the entire page.

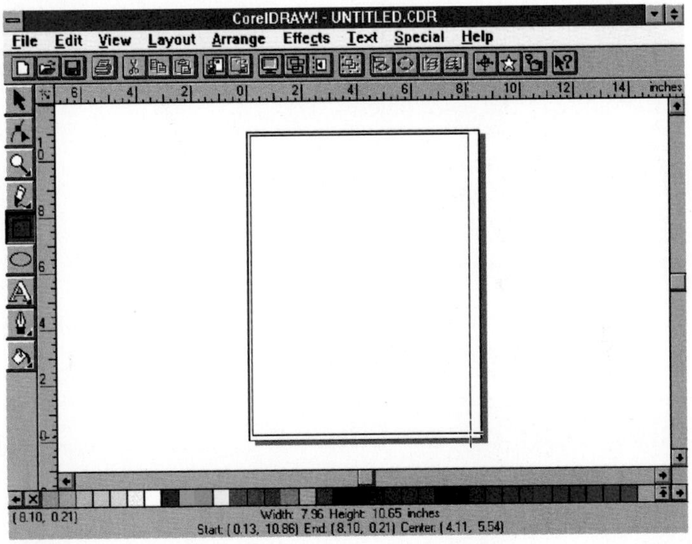

2 Open the **Fill** flyout and click the **Texture Fill** tool.

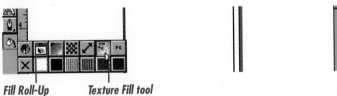

Fill Roll-Up *Texture Fill tool*

***** The Texture Fill dialog box is displayed.

3 Choose Styles from the Texture Library drop-down list.

4 Choose a fill from the Texture list.

✳ We chose Mineral, Fractal 3 Colors, and changed the color of the second mineral to turquoise by clicking the second color button and then clicking Turquoise in the color palette.

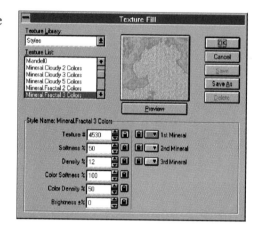

5 Choose OK.

Curving Text

This lesson includes something fun and easy—placing text on a curve. We'll place the text along a circle and a wavy line.

Placing Text on an Ellipse

First, we'll place text on an ellipse.

1 Click the Artistic Text tool.

2 Click on the middle-right side of the page to place the cursor.

3 Type Fonts & Styles.

Artistic Text tool

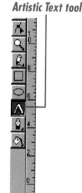

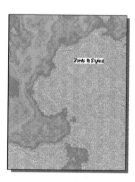

4 Click the **Ellipse** tool.

5 Hold down Ctrl, press the left mouse button, and drag the ellipse until you make a circle about the size you see in the illustration. Then release Ctrl and the mouse button.

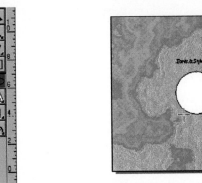

6 Click the **Pick** tool.

7 Click the text to select it.

8 Drag any of the sizing handles to stretch the text from the left to right of the circle you drew. The text remains selected.

9 Press Shift and click the circle to select it.

Stretch from here... ...to here

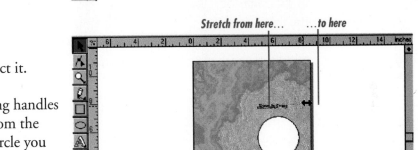

Now place the text along the circle.

1 Open the **Text** menu and choose **Fit Text To Path**.

✳ The Fit Text To Path roll-up opens.

2 Click the down arrow next to **ABC** to see the different ways you can have the text curved along the outline of the circle.

3 Select the method for placing the text on the line. We selected the top row of **ABC**.

4 Click the down arrow next to
qrs to see the different ways
you can place the text above,
on, or below the outline.

5 Select the placement for the
text in relation to the outline.
We selected the top row of **qrs**.

6 Select the place on the circle
where you want the text placed
by clicking on the divided circle image in the middle of the
roll-up. We clicked the bottom
of the circle.

7 Click **Apply**.

The text is matched to the circle. Unfortunately, this isn't the result we
wanted, but since the objects are still selected and the roll-up is still open, it
can be easily modified.

1 Change the portion of the
circle where the text is to be
placed by clicking on the top
portion of the circle in the **Fit
Text To Path** roll-up.

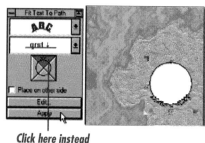

Click here instead

* If you want to make any
other changes in the roll-up,
do it now.

2 Click **Apply**.

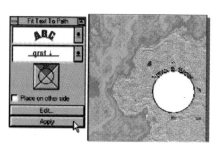

3 Delete the circle, since you no longer need it. Click outside the page to deselect both objects, then click on the circle to select it.

4 Press **Del**.

Placing Text on a Line

Let's try placing text on a wavy line:

1 Click the **Artistic Text** tool.

2 Click on the lower-left side of the page to place the cursor.

3 Type **Working With Type**.

4 Click **Freehand** tool.

5 Draw a wavy line along the bottom of the page by dragging the **Freehand** tool.

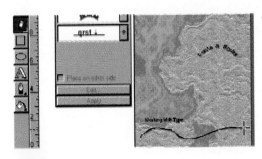

6 Click the **Pick** tool.

7 Click the text to select it.

8 Drag any of the sizing handles to stretch the text from the beginning to the end of the line you drew.

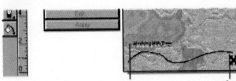

Drag the text from here...   *...to here*

9   Press Shift and click the line to select both objects.

10 In the Fit Text To Path roll-up, click in the ABC and qrs boxes to select the way you want the text placed on the line.

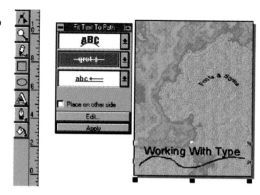

✳ A third option is displayed beside abc. This lets you place the text on the beginning, middle, or end of the line.

11 Click the center option.

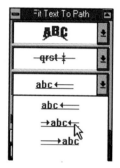

12 Choose Apply.

You won't be needing this roll-up for a while, so move it out of your way.

1 Click the arrow in the upper-right corner of the Text roll-up to roll it up.

2 Drag the roll-up to the side of the window.

Delete the line, since you no longer need it.

1 Click outside the page to deselect both objects, then click on the line to select it.

2 Press Del.

54

Changing Fonts and Styles

You're ready to learn how to modify text by changing the font, point size, attributes, and justification. You'll type text first, then edit it.

1 Click the **Artistic Text** tool.

2 Click about 2 ½ inches from the top of the page, near the left side, to place the cursor, then type **CorelDRAW 5**.

To change characteristics of all the text you just typed:

1 Click the **Pick** tool.

✳ The text is selected; you can now modify it.

2 Open the **Text** menu and choose **Text Roll-Up**.

✳ You've used the Text roll-up before to center text. You can also change the font, justification, size, and style from this roll-up.

Pick tool

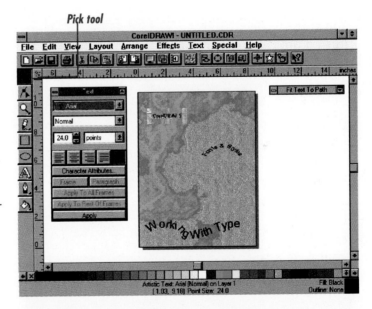

3 Open the **Typeface** drop-down list and select a font.

✳ When you highlight a font, a sample is displayed in the box on the right. We chose Palm Springs.

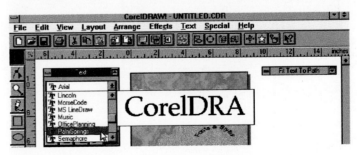

4 Change the Style to Bold.

5 Change the Size to 80 points.

6 Click the Center Justification button if not already selected.

✱ This setting causes text to be centered within its selection box, not within the page.

7 Click Apply.

8 Drag the text to position it on the page.

✱ You won't be needing this roll-up for a while, so move it out of your way as described earlier.

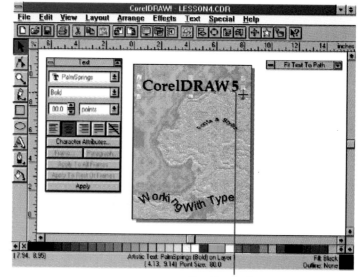

Drag the text here

Editing Text

Now we'll modify the text Working With Type, which you typed earlier.

✱ The Pick tool is still selected.

1 Click Working With Type to select it.

2 Open the Text menu and choose Edit Text.

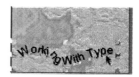

✳ The Edit Text dialog box is displayed. The cursor is at the end of the text.

Press *Backspace* to delete Type

3 Press Backspace until the word **Type** is deleted.

4 Type the word **Text**.

Then type Text

5 Click before the letter **W** in **Working** and drag the mouse to the end of **Text** to select the words **Working With Text**.

Once you have the text entered the way you want it, you can modify its characteristics.

1 Click **Character** at the bottom of the **Edit Text** dialog box.

✳ The Character Attributes dialog box is opened. You can modify characteristics of the text from here.

2 In the **Fonts** list box, highlight and preview fonts until you find the one you want, then select it. We chose SwitzerlandBlack.

3 Change the Size to 32 points.

4 In the **Alignment** box, select **Center**.

5 Click **OK** in the **Character Attributes** dialog box.

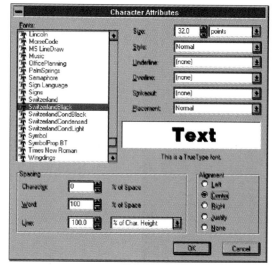

6 Click **OK** in the **Edit Text** dialog box.

7 Drag the text into position on the page, dragging the selection box as well.

Drag the text here

Now magnify the text CorelDRAW 5 so you can modify the individual letter **C**.

1 Click the **Zoom** tool, then click the **Zoom In** tool on the flyout menu.

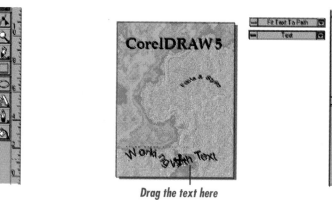

2 Using the magnifying glass cursor, drag from the top left of the text to the bottom right, then release the mouse button.

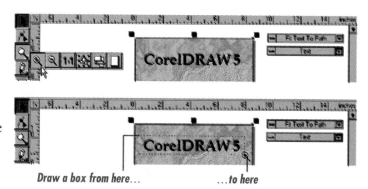

Draw a box from here...   *...to here*

✳ This draws a marquee selection box around the text. The text is magnified.

3 Click the **Shape** tool.

4 Click **CorelDRAW 5**.

Shape tool

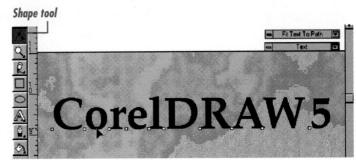

✱ You can clearly see the nodes before each letter. By double-clicking on a letter's node, you can modify the letter without changing any of the other text.

Let's modify the **C**.

1 Double-click the node to the left of the **C**.

Double-click here to modify the C

✱ The Character Attributes dialog box is displayed.

2 In the **Fonts** list box, highlight and preview fonts until you find the one you want, then select it. We chose Lincoln.

3 Change the **Size** to **140 points**.

4 Click **OK**.

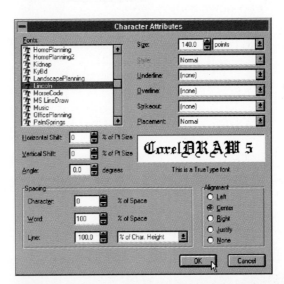

5 Click the **Zoom** tool, then click the **Zoom To Page** tool.

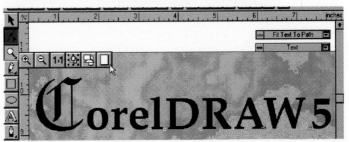

For a more interesting effect, let's place a rectangle behind the letter *C* in *CorelDRAW* and fill it with a Linear Fill.

1 Click the **Rectangle** tool.

2 Draw a rectangle that covers the letter C.

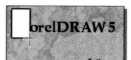

3 Click the **Pick** tool to select the rectangle.

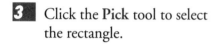

4 Open the **Fill** flyout and click the **Texture Fill** tool.

5 Choose **Styles** from the Texture **Library** drop-down list.

6 Choose a fill from the **Texture** list. We chose Threads Rainbow.

7 Choose **OK**.

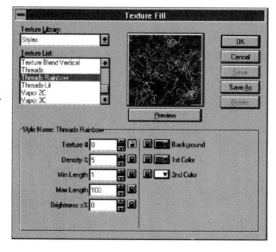

8 Open the **Arrange** menu and choose **Order**, then choose **Back One**.

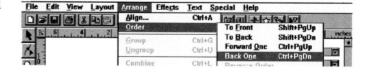

9 Click the **Shape** tool.

10 Click anywhere on the word CorelDRAW, then click the node to the left of the C.

11 Click a color in the color palette.

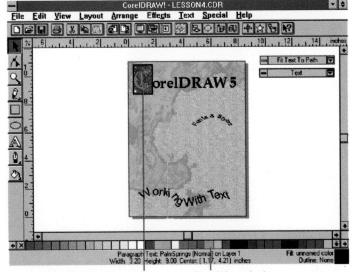

Click the node here first... ...then click a color here

Including Paragraph Text

You can create text with most popular word processing programs and include it, without retyping it, in a drawing. We have a small paragraph, created with Word for Windows, which we'll import. You can use any text you have handy.

NOTE

There is a 8000 character limit per paragraph on the amount of text you can import at one time.

To import text from another file, do the following:

1 Open the **File** menu and choose **Import**.

✱ The Import Files dialog box is opened.

2 Click the down arrow in the **List Files Of Type** box, then select the name and version you are using.

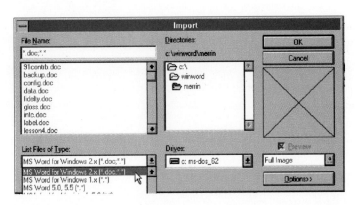

✳ We chose MS Word for Windows (*.doc, *.*).

3 Change the path in the **Directories** list box, until the directory that contains the file is selected.

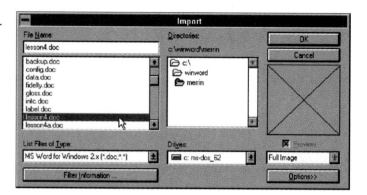

4 In the **File Name** list box, click the name of the file you want to bring in.

5 Click **OK**.

✳ The text is placed on the page in a frame.

6 Resize the frame by dragging the sizing handles.

✳ Our frame is about 1 ½ inches wide by 5 ½ inches high.

7 Drag the frame to the left side of the page.

✳ The frame containing the text should still be selected.

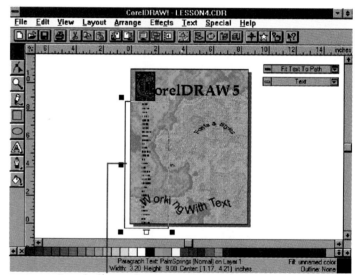

Drag the frame to here

NOTE

Because of the way CorelDRAW's defaults are set, you may not see the text in the frame, or it may not fit in the frame until you make some modifications to the text and frame.

Modifying Paragraph Text

With the Text roll-up, you can easily modify the paragraph text that you just imported.

1 Click the down arrow in the Text roll-up to open it.

2 In the **Typeface** drop-down list, select a font for your text. We chose PalmSprings.

3 Change the **Size** to **13 points**.

4 Click the **Full Justification** button.

5 Click the **Paragraph** button.

✱ The Paragraph dialog box is opened and the Spacing tab is highlighted at the top.

6 Open the **Line** drop-down list and choose **% Of Char. Height**.

7 Type **125** in the **Line** text box.

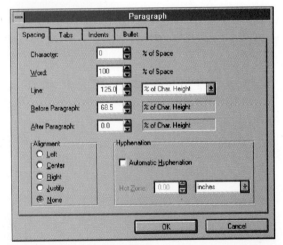

8 Click the **Indents** tab.

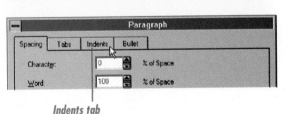

Indents tab

9 Change the **First Line** and **Rest Of Line** entries to **0**.

10 Change the **Left Margin** and **Right Margin** entries to **0**.

 This will cause the text to fill the frame once the selections are applied.

11 Click **OK**.

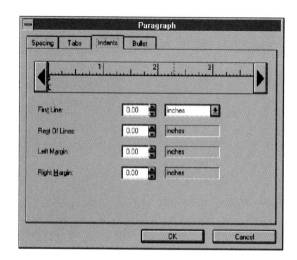

12 Click **Apply To Frame**.

NOTE

If your text still doesn't fit in the frame, you can try reducing the point size and line spacing. You can also make the frame larger until all the text is visible.

Entering Paragraph Text

If you didn't have your text already entered into another program, you could easily enter it right into your drawing. To try this feature out, you'll delete the frame which contains the imported text, and use the Paragraph tool to enter the text onto the drawing page:

1 Click the **Pick** tool.

2 Click on the frame which contains the imported text.

3 Press Del.

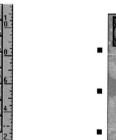

✳ The frame is deleted.

Now type the text into your drawing:

1 Click and hold the **Artistic Text** tool to open the flyout. Click the **Paragraph Text** tool.

2 Click the cursor below the **C** in **CorelDRAW 5**.

✳ As you click, a frame is placed on the page.

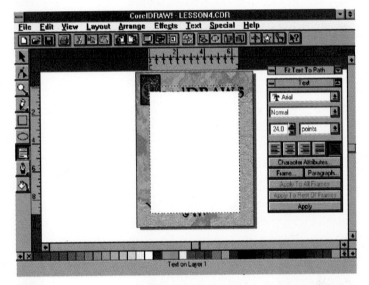

3 Type a paragraph of two or three sentences in the frame.

4 Now follow steps 2–12 in the previous set of steps to modify the paragraph text so it looks like the imported text.

 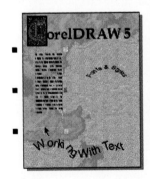 

Modifying Several Items

If you have several text objects in a drawing and you want to apply the same attributes to them, you can select them all and then change their attributes.

Let's duplicate the text **Fonts & Styles** to try this out.

1 Click the **Pick** tool.

2 Click the text **Fonts & Styles**.

3 Open the **Edit** menu and choose **Duplicate**.

4 Open the **Edit** menu again and choose **Repeat Duplicate** until there are five text objects in all.

✳ Four copies of the object are pasted on the page, slightly above and to the right of the first. The top object is selected.

5 Drag the top object below the original.

6 Click each duplicate and drag it below the previous one, until it matches the drawing.

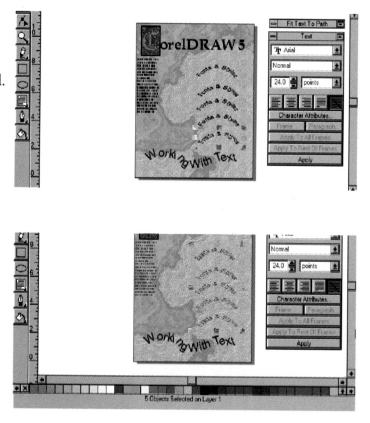

✳ The last text object is still selected.

7 Press Shift and click each text object to select them all.

8 Click a color in the color palette.

9 In the **Text** roll-up, select **Casablanca** from the **Typeface** drop-down list.

10 Select **Bold-Italic** from the **Style** drop-down list.

11 Change the **Size** to **51 points**.

12 Click **Apply** to apply your selections to the text.

NOTE

When you've selected one text object with the Pick tool, you can then press Shift and click additional text objects to select several and modify their attributes at the same time.

Finishing Touches

As always, we recommend you save and print your work. You may also want to try achieving some different effects with text before you go on to Lesson 5.

Our finished design is shown. We added the following touches:

- A rectangle behind the paragraph text. The rectangle is filled with pink. You'll need to use the Order command on the Arrange menu, and the Back One option to move it behind the text.

- The text **Lesson 4** in Gatineau Italic, 104 points.

- A pie wedge behind the text **Lesson 4**.

- Several straight and wavy lines.

We also changed the font and color for each Fonts & Styles. We left the bottom object as Casablanca and changed the others (from top to bottom) to the following fonts: Switzerland Condensed Light, Switzerland Condensed Black, Freeport Normal, and PalmSprings Bold. And, we changed the color of each.

LESSON

5 Printing, Importing, and Exporting Files and Graphics

20 MINUTES

Although you've been printing the drawings you've created, there are some additional printing capabilities you haven't tried yet. In this lesson, you'll learn how to use some of the available print options and how to save a file for a service bureau. You'll also try some file import, export, and clipboard techniques and work with a template.

Using Print Options

Begin the lesson by opening the file you created in Lesson 2, **lesson2.cdr**. The drawing included linear fills, so it is a good sample for these printing steps.

1 Open the File menu and choose Open.

* The Open Drawing dialog box is displayed.

2 In the Directories list box, double-click the directory where you've saved your files. If you aren't sure, try the **draw** directory in **corel50** first.

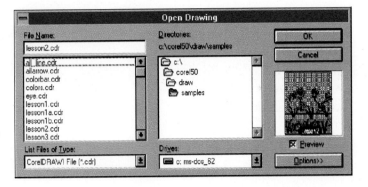

3 Click **lesson2.cdr** in the File Name list box, then click OK.

Try changing the options CorelDRAW uses when you print at your own printer.

NOTE

All the printing options are not available if the printer you have installed is not a PostScript printer.

1 Open the File menu and select **Print**.

✳ The Print dialog box is displayed.

2 Click **Options**.

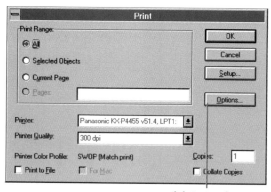

Click Options here

3 Select **Preview Image**, if necessary.

4 In the **Width** text box, enter 75%.

5 In the **Height** text box, enter 75%.

✳ If Maintain Aspect is checked, the Height box will be dimmed, and you'll only need to enter a value for the Width.

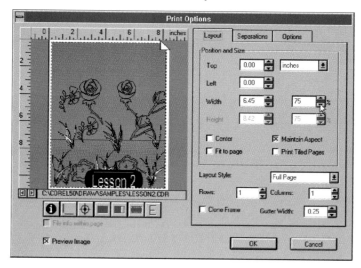

6 Select the **Options** tab.

7 Decrease the number of Fountain Steps to 20.

8 Click **OK** twice.

Click Options here

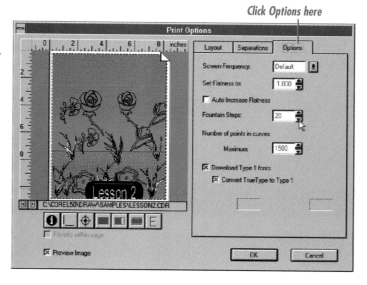

The Printing File dialog box is displayed. Your drawing is printed.

NOTE

If you use the Scale option to reduce the size of the drawing, it will help speed up the printing. When you are printing for your own use in order to see a work in progress, this will save some time. It is also useful for creating a proof of a drawing that is too large for your printer to handle.

NOTE

The Fountain Steps option determines how many bands a PostScript printer will print for each fountain fill in a drawing. If you set it for a low number, it will increase the printing speed, but decrease the quality of your output.

Printing to a File

Next, you'll prepare a file for printing from another computer or for delivery to a service bureau.

1 Open the File menu and choose Print.

✱ The Print dialog box is displayed.

2 Select Print To File.

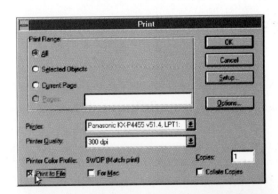

3 Click OK.

✱ The Print To File dialog box is displayed.

71

NOTE

To print the file later at a service bureau, you'll need to select the printer which the service bureau will be using. You can install and select another printer using the Windows Control Panel. Refer to the Microsoft Windows *User's Guide* for more information.

✳ lesson2.prn is shown in the File Name text box.

4 Click OK.

Your drawing is printed to a file named **lesson2.prn**. This file can be printed from another computer or delivered to a service bureau for printing.

Exporting a File from Corel

You'll probably want to include some of your drawings in documents you create in another application (for example, a desktop publishing application other than Corel Ventura or a word processing program). You'll need to save your drawings in a file format that is compatible with the other application. The Export command lets you do this.

NOTE

You do not need to export CorelDRAW files in a different format to include them in a document you are desktop publishing with Corel Ventura. Corel Ventura lets you easily include drawings you've created and saved with CorelDRAW.

1 Open the File menu and choose Export.

✳ The Export File dialog box is displayed.

2 Open the List Files Of Type list box and select EPS (Placeable), *.eps.

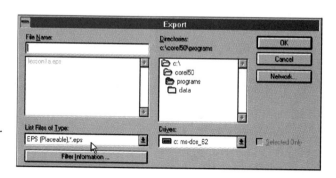

3 Type the file name **lesson2.eps** in the **File Name** text box.

4 Click **OK**.

✱ The Export EPS dialog box is displayed.

5 Check **Include Header**.

✱ Image Header allows you to see the image when you import it into another application. Otherwise, you may just see an "X" on-screen in the other program, instead of the image.

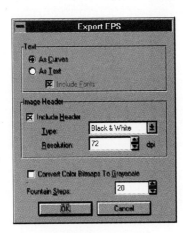

6 In **Fountain Steps**, enter **20**.

7 Click **OK**.

✱ A dialog box tells you CorelDRAW is exporting the file.

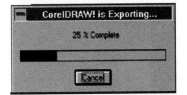

You can open the new file in any application that imports EPS files.

NOTE

You can use Encapsulated PostScript files with most word processing and desktop publishing applications. However, if you want to export your drawings for use in WordPerfect, you should choose the option WordPerfect Graphic *.wpg in the List Files Of Type drop-down list, in the Export File dialog box.

Exporting a File for Corel PHOTO-PAINT

There are times when you'll want to bring a CorelDRAW drawing into Corel PHOTO-PAINT to achieve some effects not available in CorelDRAW. Or, you may sometimes begin a drawing by using CorelDRAW objects and then complete it with Corel PHOTO-PAINT. In either case, you'll have to export your drawing in PCX format from CorelDRAW before you can open it in Corel PHOTO-PAINT.

1 Open the **File** menu and choose **Export**.

* The Export File dialog box is displayed.

2 Open the **List Files Of Type** box and select **Paintbrush *.pcx**.

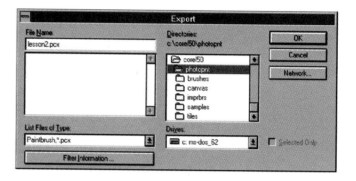

3 Type **lesson2.pcx** in the **File Name** text box.

4 Click **OK**.

* The Bitmap Export box is displayed.

5 Select **256 colors**.

6 Under **Size**, choose **1024 × 768**.

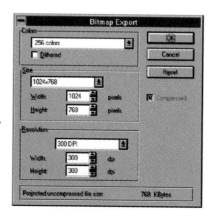

7 Under **Resolution**, choose **300 dpi**.

8 Click **OK**.

* You'll see a dialog box that tells you CorelDRAW is exporting the file.

You can open the file in any application that accepts PCX files; for example, in Windows Paintbrush.

Using a Template

CorelDRAW includes special files called *templates* to help you speed up your work. Templates are available for items such as brochures, newsletters, business cards, invitations, and menus. These templates already have the page or pages set up, and come with sample text and art so you can easily see how they are laid out. You'll open a template in this exercise and then bring in alternate art and text in the next exercise. Begin with a new drawing page.

1 Open the **File** menu and choose **New From Template**.

* If you've made changes to **lesson2.cdr**, you'll be prompted to save the changes. Click **No**.

* The New From Template dialog box is displayed.

* CorelDRAW Template (*.cdt) will be displayed in the List Files Of Type box.

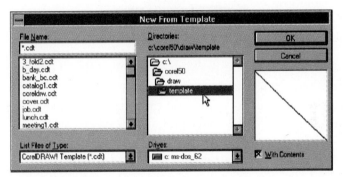

2 If necessary, in the **Directories** list box, double-click the **corel50** directory, double-click the **draw** directory, then double-click the **template** directory.

3 Select **news_box.cdt** from the CD-ROM drive (or any template you'd like to try using) in the **File Name** list box.

4 Select **With Contents**.

5 Click **OK**.

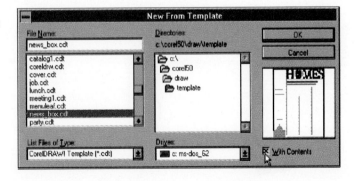

✳ A sample three-page newsletter is opened on the drawing page.

6 To see pages 2 and 3 of the newsletter, click the right arrow in the left corner of the window.

Click here to see the next page

7 To return to page 1, click the left arrow in the left corner of the window.

Modifying a Template

You can modify this drawing as you would any drawing you created yourself. You can also paste art you've copied to the Clipboard from other drawings or applications. And you can import art, such as clip art and PCX files you've created with Corel PHOTO-PAINT.

First, make room for some of your own art and text.

1 Click the **Pick** tool.

2 Click the first column of text.

3 Press Shift and click the other columns to select them all.

Press Shift and click here...

...and here... ...and here

4 Press Del.

* The selected items are deleted.

5 Delete the banner and art on the first page by clicking each item to select it and then pressing Del.

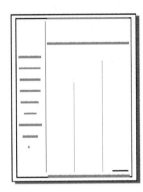

You now have room to add your own art and text.

Copying with the Clipboard

Let's open the drawing from the last lesson and insert some of the text into the newsletter. You can easily do this with the Windows Clipboard.

1 Open the **File** menu and choose **Open**.

2 If necessary, click **No** when you see the **Save Changes To news_box.cdt** prompt.

3 Click **Yes** when you see the **Save current changes?** prompt.

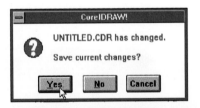

* The Save Drawing dialog box is displayed.

4 Type **lesson5.cdr** in the File Name text box and click **OK**.

✳ The Open Drawing dialog box is displayed.

5 If necessary, in the **Directories** list box, double-click the directory where you've saved your files. Try the directory where you found **lesson2.cdr** first.

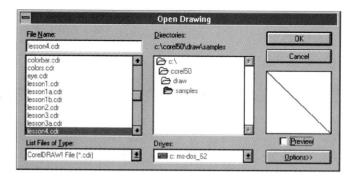

6 Click **lesson4.cdr** in the File Name list box, and the drawing you created for Lesson 4 is opened.

Now select several items to copy.

1 Click the Pick tool.

2 Click the paragraph of text.

Click here first

3 Press Shift and click each **Fonts & Styles** to select them all.

4 Press Shift and click **CorelDRAW 5** at the top to select it also.

*Press **Shift** and click here*

5 Open the **Edit** menu and choose **Copy**.

6 Open the **File** menu and select **lesson5.cdr** from the bottom.

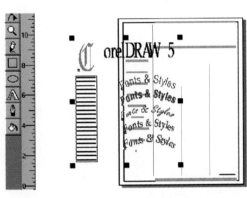

7 Click **No** at the **Save current changes?** prompt.

8 Open the **Edit** menu and choose **Paste**.

✳ All the copied objects are pasted to the page, and all are selected.

9 Click outside the drawing page to deselect them all.

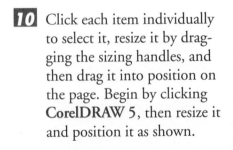

10 Click each item individually to select it, resize it by dragging the sizing handles, and then drag it into position on the page. Begin by clicking **CorelDRAW 5**, then resize it and position it as shown.

Click and drag to here

NOTE

You can copy any objects from one drawing to another by selecting them, choosing Copy, then Paste when you have the destination displayed on the drawing page.

11 Move and resize the other
items to fit on the page.

Importing a File

You've already imported clip art files into a CorelDRAW drawing. Now you'll
import a PCX file and include it in your newsletter.

1 Open the **File** menu and
choose **Import**.

✳ The Import dialog box is
displayed.

2 From the **List Files Of Type**
box, select **Paintbrush (*.pcx)**.

3 If necessary, select your
CD-ROM drive from the
Drives drop-down list.

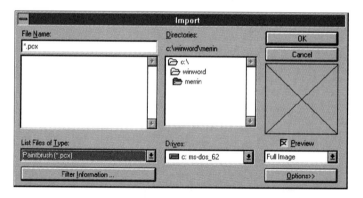

4 In the **Directories** list box,
double-click **corel50**, double-
click **photopnt**, then double-
click **samples**.

5 In the **File Name** list box,
click **apple.pcx**.

6 Click **Preview** to see the file
before it is opened.

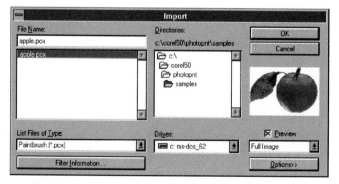

7 Click **OK**.

* The apple is placed on your page and selected.

8 Resize it by dragging the sizing handles, and then drag it into position on the page as shown.

← Drag in from here..

...then drag to here →

Finishing Touches

Finish this lesson by adding text and pictures to the template; you already have the skills to create a newsletter of your own with CorelDRAW. You might want to open several different templates so you see what's available to you. Spend as much or as little time as you have and use your imagination, clip art, and symbols.

20 MINUTES

LESSON 6

Maximizing Your Results

Now that you've been working with CorelDRAW, there are probably some changes you'd like to make to the default settings; for example, to change the width of the outline pen and the fill given to objects when you create them. You are also ready to use more of CorelDRAW's on-screen guides to help speed up your work. And, this is a good time to begin using the ribbon bar, if you haven't been doing so already.

This lesson gives you the opportunity to set CorelDRAW up in the way that works best for you. It is a little different from the other lessons in that you won't be creating a generic design that can be used in business. You'll be creating a chart that would be appropriate for use with children, but the tools you'll be using can be applied to all your drawings.

Using the Ribbon Bar

The ribbon bar has several buttons that open roll-ups and dialog boxes, which you've been using throughout the first five lessons. The buttons duplicate the functions of many commands on the menus and can be used instead of those commands.

Ribbon bar —
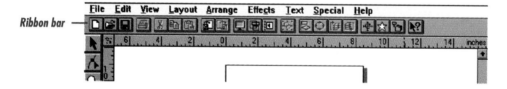

NOTE

You can use either menus or buttons to access CorelDRAW's features, depending on your preference. Most people prefer to use the graphic buttons when available, once they are familiar with what each does.

You can find out what a button does by doing the following:

✳ Place the mouse pointer over the button and hold briefly to see a label. Look at the bottom of the screen to see a description.

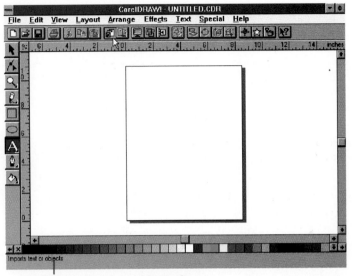

Look here to see what each button does

When you find the button you want, click it.

We'll show you a picture of each button you need to use in this lesson, to help you get started.

Setting Up the Page and Window

First, let's change the page orientation.

1 Open the **Layout** menu and choose **Page Setup**.

✳ The Page Setup dialog box is displayed and the Size tab is selected.

2 Select **Landscape**.

3 Click the **Display** tab to reveal the **Display** options.

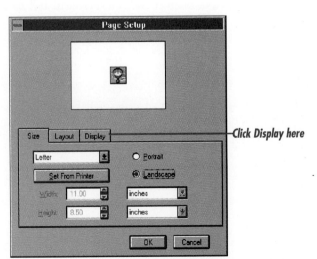

Click Display here

4 Select **Paper Color**.

* The Paper Color color palette opens.

5 Select a color. We selected a shade of blue.

6 Choose **OK**.

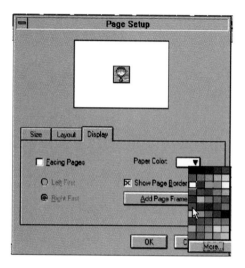

NOTE

The Paper Color dialog box is similar to the Uniform Fill dialog box. If you were going to print your document on colored stock instead of white stock, this is where you'd indicate the color. When CorelDRAW prints, it does not print the color background. But by selecting a color here, you'll be able to see how your background color matches the rest of the colors you use in your design.

Changing Outline and Fill Defaults

Let's change the defaults for the Outline Pen and Fill so the objects require less modification when they are created.

1 Click the **Outline** tool, then click the **Outline Dialog** tool in the **Outline** flyout menu.

✳ The first **Outline Pen** dialog box is opened. This dialog box is opened by clicking the Outline Dialog tool when no object is selected. You can change the outline for all the objects before you create them.

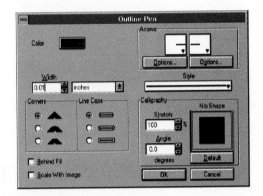

2 Click **Graphic**.

3 Click **OK**.

✳ Another Outline Pen dialog box is opened.

4 Change the width to **0.01 inches.**

5 Click **OK**.

A similar process changes the fill for new objects.

1 Click the **Fill** tool, then click the **Fill Color** tool in the **Fill** flyout menu.

✳ The first Uniform Fill dialog box is opened. This dialog box is opened by clicking the Fill Color tool when no object is selected. You can change the fill for all the objects you are going to create. This is often quicker than changing the fill for each object individually.

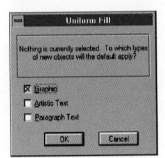

2 Click **Graphic**.

3 Click OK.

✳ Another Uniform Fill dialog box is opened.

4 In the Show list box, select CMYK Color Model.

5 Change the color to White by clicking white in the color palette or setting C (cyan), M (magenta), Y (yellow), and K (black) to 0.

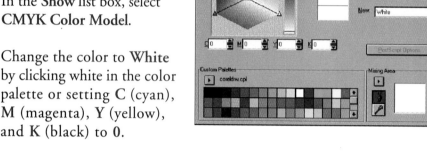

6 Click OK.

Using Guidelines

Let's add a guideline to help you align the objects you are going to add.

1 Open the Layout menu and choose Guidelines Setup.

✳ The Guidelines Setup dialog box is opened.

2 Click Horizontal Guidelines.

3 Select inches from the drop-down list, if necessary.

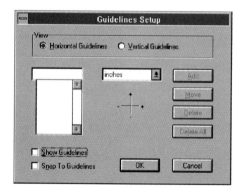

4 Click Snap To Guidelines.

5 Click Show Guidelines.

6 In the text box, type 1.25.

7 Click Add.

8 Click OK.

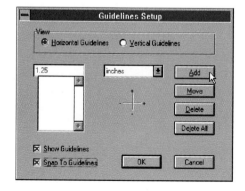

✱ The guideline is displayed on the drawing page.

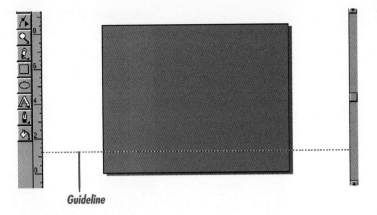

Guideline

Adding Symbols and Clip Art

The objects you'll include in the chart are all either clip art or symbols. First, bring in the symbols.

1 Click the **Symbols Roll-Up** button in the ribbon bar.

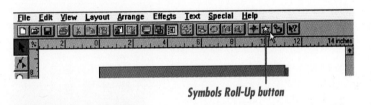

Symbols Roll-Up button

✱ The Symbols roll-up is displayed. The drop-down list shows the categories of symbols you installed.

2 Choose **Food** from the drop-down list.

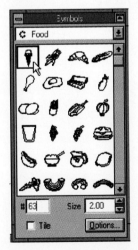

NOTE

Remember that if you chose a custom rather than a full install and did not install all the symbols, they will not be displayed in the drop-down list.

3 Drag the ice cream cone (**#63**) symbol from the roll-up to the editing window.

4 Drag the container of milk (**#88**) symbol from the roll-up to the editing window.

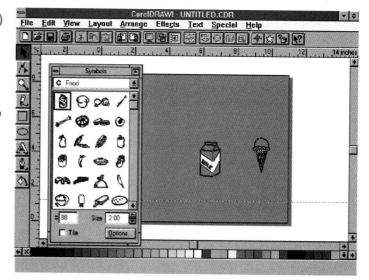

✱ Remember to use the scroll bar to display all the symbols in this category. Look at the bottom of the roll-up to see the symbol number. Or, type the numbers **63** and then **88** in the # text box to select the symbol.

5 Repeat steps 3 and 4 to bring in two more symbols in the **Food** category: cheese (**#56**) and meat (**#119**).

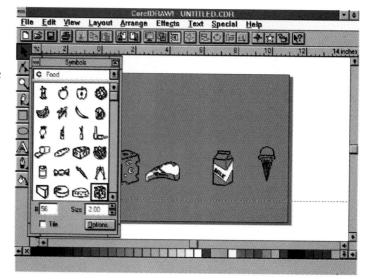

6 Double-click the **Close** box on the **Symbols** roll-up.

Now bring in the last item from the clip art on disk.

1 Click the **Import** button in the ribbon bar.

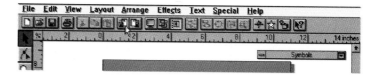

✳ The Import dialog box is displayed. Make sure the drive letter for your CD-ROM drive is shown in the Drive list box.

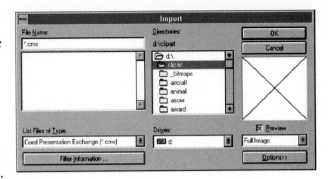

2 Open the **List Files Of Type** drop-down list and select **Corel Presentation Exchange (*.cmx)**.

3 Double-click the **Corel50** directory to make the **clipart** directory visible, if necessary. Scroll down the **Directories** list box using the scroll bar until you see the **clipart** directory, then double-click it.

4 Scroll down the list box again to the **animals** directory, then double-click it.

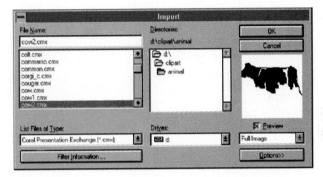

✳ You'll see a list of the files in the **clipart\creature** directory in the File Name box.

5 Scroll the box until you see **cow2.cmx**, then double-click it.

✳ That's the first file you'll be importing to your drawing.

6 Click **OK**.

✳ The dialog box closes and a picture of a cow is on your drawing page.

7 Drag any of the sizing handles in to make it smaller.

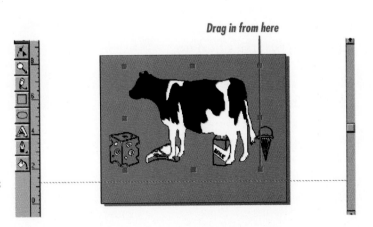

Drag in from here

✳ You now have all the art for your chart.

Positioning with a Guideline

Let's resize and position the clip art and symbols.

1 Click the **Pick** tool.

2 Resize the ice cream cone, then reposition it by dragging it near the guideline.

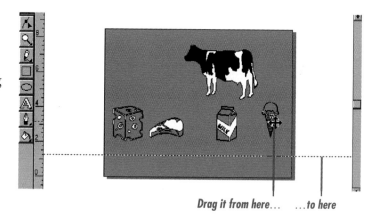

Drag it from here...   ...to here

✳ You'll notice it seems to "catch" on the guideline.

3 Resize the other food objects, then reposition them by dragging them near the guideline.

4 Resize the cow and place it near the middle of the page.

✳ You'll notice that if you aren't dragging an object near the guideline, your ability to position the object is not affected.

Moving a Guideline

Now let's move the guideline to the top of the page to position some objects there.

1 Open the **Layout** menu and choose **Guidelines Setup**.

* The Guidelines Setup dialog box is opened.

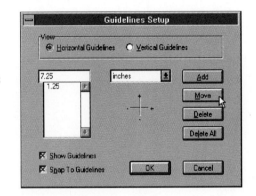

2 In the text box, set the inches to **7.25**.

3 Click **Move**.

4 Click **OK**.

Now you'll select the cow and duplicate it, fill the copy with a brown color, and put it in the corner.

* The cow is already selected.

1 Open the **Edit** menu and choose **Duplicate**.

* A copy of the cow is pasted on top of the original.

2 Drag the new cow to the upper-right corner and resize it so it is much smaller.

3 Click on a shade of brown in the color palette.

Drag the new cow here...

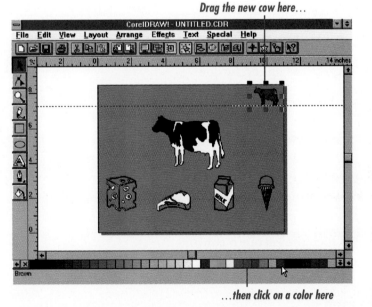

...then click on a color here

Make another duplicate for the other corner using the following steps.

1 Click the **Transform Roll-Up** button in the ribbon bar.

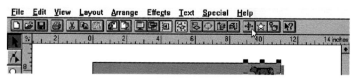

✱ The Transform roll-up opens.

2 Click the **Mirror** button.

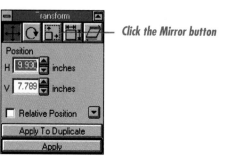

Click the Mirror button

3 Under **Scale**, enter 100 for both **H** and **V**.

4 Click the **Horizontal Mirror** button.

5 Click **Apply To Duplicate**.

Horizontal Mirror button

6 Drag the new cow to the upper-left corner.

7 Close the roll-up by double-clicking its **Close** box.

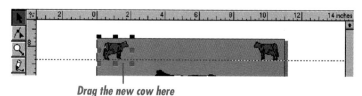

Drag the new cow here

Both cows should be on the guideline and positioned evenly.

Removing a Guideline

We no longer need the guideline, so let's remove it.

1 Open the **Layout** menu and choose **Guidelines Setup**.

✳ The Guidelines Setup dialog box is opened. The ruler position is set to 7.25 inches.

2 Click Del.

3 Click OK.

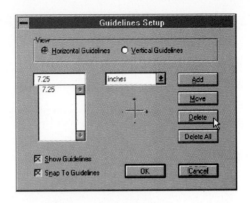

Changing the View

No matter how fast your computer is, you will probably need to speed up the time it takes CorelDRAW to redraw the screen sometimes. Changing the view to Wireframe view will help on these occasions.

1 Click the **Wireframe** button in the ribbon bar.

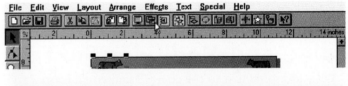

✳ You will only see a black and white outline of your drawing.

2 Click the **Full-Screen Preview** button in the ribbon bar.

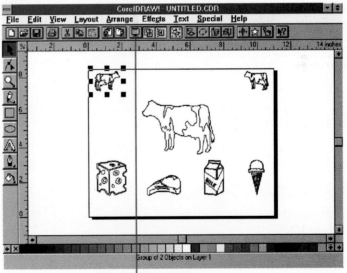

Full-Screen Preview button

✳ You'll see your drawing page in full color, but you won't see anything off to the side of your drawing page. You cannot make any changes to your drawing in Preview mode.

3 Press Esc to return to Wireframe view.

Try working in Wireframe view for a while, to determine if it speeds up your overall productivity in CorelDRAW.

Adding and Modifying Text

Let's add some text to the chart. Then you'll learn a style shortcut.

1 Click the **Artistic Text** tool.

2 Click beneath the picture of the cheese to place the cursor.

3 Type the word **cheese**.

Click here and type

4 Click beneath each picture at the bottom of the page and type a label.

Placing Text on a Path

Next, we'll add text to a path. You learned how to do this in Lesson 4, but we'll review the steps quickly here.

1   Click off the page to place the cursor.

2   Type **What foods come from cows?**

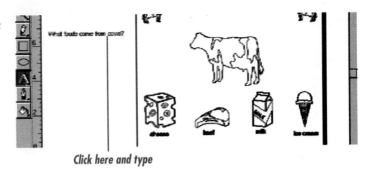

Click here and type

3   Click the **Ellipse** tool.

4   Hold down Ctrl, press the left mouse button, and drag the ellipse until you make a circle about five inches in diameter. Then release Ctrl and the mouse button.

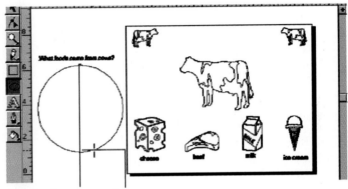

Drag from here... ...to here

5   Click the **Pick** tool.

✱   The circle is selected.

6   Press Shift and click the text to select it while keeping the circle selected.

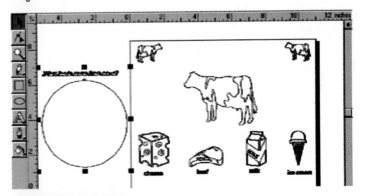

7   Open the **Text** menu and choose **Fit Text To Path**.

✱   The **Fit Text To Path** roll-up opens. We used the default settings.

8   Click **Apply**.

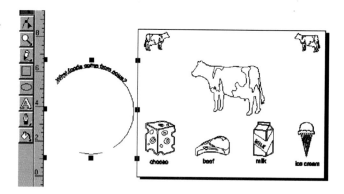

❋ The text is placed on the circle.

9 Close the roll-up by double-clicking its **Close** box.

10 Select just the circle and press Del to delete it.

11 Select and drag the text so it is above the cow.

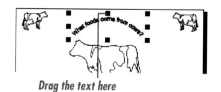

Drag the text here

Copying Attributes

Now that all the text is in, you can change the font, style, and size easily.

1 Select the word **cheese**.

2 Open the **Text** menu and choose **Text Roll-Up**.

❋ The **Text** roll-up opens.

3 Modify the text by using the **Text** roll-up. We changed the font to Freeport and the size to 54 points.

4 Click **Apply**.

5 Choose a color from the color palette.

✳ You won't see the color on your drawing page, but you will see the color on the right side of the status line.

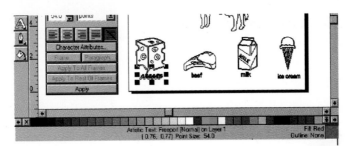

The color shows here

6 Close the roll-up by double-clicking its **Close** box.

Apply the style you've created to the other text.

1 Click the **Pick** tool, then se-lect the rest of the text on the page, using the Shift-and-click technique.

2 Open the **Edit** menu and choose **Copy Attributes From**.

✳ The Copy Attributes dialog box is displayed.

3 Check **Outline Pen**, **Fill**, and **Text Attributes**.

4 Click **OK**.

✳ The cursor changes to an arrow.

5 Click the arrow on the word **cheese**.

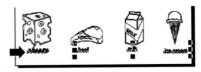

All the other text on the page is modified so it now matches the style of the text to which you pointed. You can't see this in Wireframe view, so switch back to Normal viewing mode.

1 Click the Wireframe button in the ribbon bar.

✳ You'll see all the objects in their selected colors.

Wireframe button

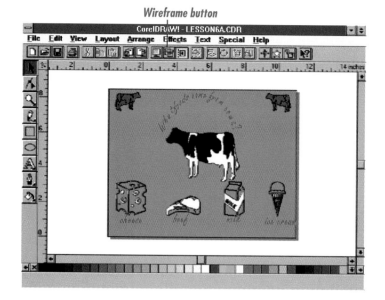

Using the Grid

Try using the grid instead of the guidelines to help you line up objects.

1 Open the Layout menu and choose Grid & Scale Setup.

✳ The Grid & Scale Setup dialog box is displayed.

2 Under Grid Frequency, change Horizontal to 4.00 per inch and Vertical to 2.00 per inch.

3 Check Show Grid.

4 Check Snap To Grid.

5 Click OK.

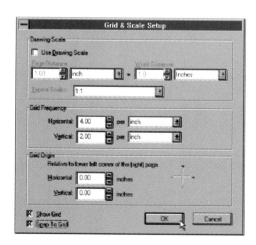

6 Try using the grid to position the text that is on the bottom of the page. Drag the text so it is aligned horizontally, using the grid to help you.

Grid

7 When you are finished, open the Layout menu and choose Snap To Grid to turn off the command.

NOTE

The Snap To Grid command affects your ability to freely move all the objects on the page, while the Snap To Guidelines command affects only those objects near the guideline.

Finishing Touches

After we used the Text tool to add question marks to the little brown cows in the corners, we used two more commands to clean things up a bit. First, we centered each text object on its associated picture. Then we grouped each object with its picture so we could move the two together freely.

1 Use the Pick tool and Shift-and-click to select the word cheese and the picture of the cheese.

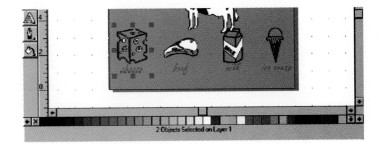

2 Click the **Align** button in the ribbon bar.

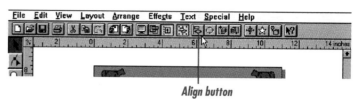

Align button

✱ The Align dialog box opens.

3 Under **Horizontally**, select **Center**.

4 Click **OK**.

5 Repeat the steps for all the text and picture pairs, including the cow and text on a curve.

NOTE

Remember to first select the item that you want moved, then open the Edit menu and choose Repeat.

6 After you've aligned the objects, select the first pair with Shift-and-click.

7 Open the **Arrange** menu and choose **Group**.

✱ This will let you move the picture and word together if you want to adjust things a bit, as we did at the end.

8 Select each text and picture pair and choose **Group**.

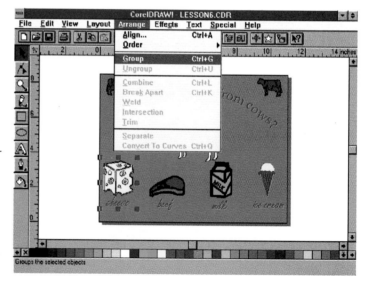

To make the symbols look as nice as the clip art, we added color to the milk container and ice cream cone. If you need a refresher on how to add color to symbols, refer back to Lesson 3.

Remember to save and print your creation when you are finished.

Managing Files with Corel MOSAIC

15 MINUTES

In Lesson 3, you used Corel MOSAIC to locate and import clip art into a CorelDRAW drawing. In this lesson, you'll use Corel MOSAIC's file management capabilities to find and organize your drawings, CorelDRAW's clip art, and the files others create and give you.

Getting Started

The Corel5 group window contains the program icons that let you start the Corel applications. This is the same window from which you launched CorelDRAW.

1 If the **Corel5** group window is not open, double-click the **Corel5** icon at the bottom of the **Program Manager** window.

2 To start **Corel MOSAIC**, double-click the **Corel MOSAIC** icon in the **Corel5** group window.

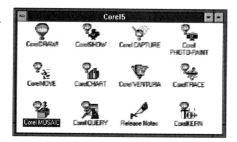

✳ The Corel MOSAIC program is launched. You'll see the Corel MOSAIC window.

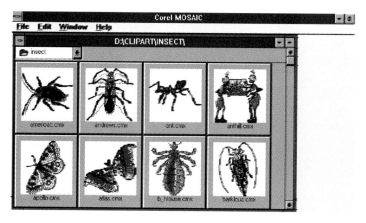

NOTE

The window does not contain tools down the left side as CorelDRAW's main window does. And, there are fewer menus and other window components to learn before you get started.

NOTE

The window contains one or more additional windows which show the directory and files you last viewed. If you have not yet taken Lesson 3 and this is the first time you are using Corel MOSAIC, no other windows are opened and the Mosaic window is empty. If you have not used Corel MOSAIC since Lesson 3, the Mosaic window shows thumbnails of all the files that are in the clipart\insect directory.

Working with Thumbnails in Corel MOSAIC

If you want to browse through a group of files to find a particular piece of art, the Mosaic window is the place to do it. With Corel MOSAIC, you can look through a directory and see a thumbnail of each of its files. If you find what you're looking for, you can open it in CorelDRAW.

Begin by locating all the drawings you've created while working on Lessons 1–6.

1 Double-click the **Close** box on any open windows.

Don't double-click here

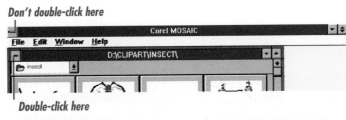

Double-click here

✳ The Mosaic window is empty.

2 Open the **File** menu and choose **Open Collection.**

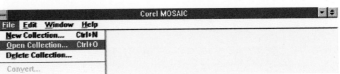

✳ The Open Collection dialog box is displayed.

3 Select All Files in the List Files Of Type drop-down list.

4 In the Directories list box, double-click the directory where you've been saving your drawing files. If you aren't sure, try double-clicking corel50 and then draw.

✳ You'll see the lesson files in the File Names box when you locate the right directory.

5 Click OK.

✳ The Mosaic window shows thumbnails of all the files in that directory.

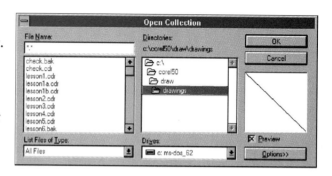

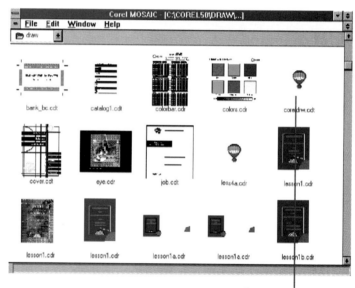

CorelDRAW program icon

NOTE

If you see a program icon instead of a thumbnail, it means that Corel MOSAIC is unable to display the image. The icon represents the program in which the image was created.

Once you've found the file you want to edit, you can open it in CorelDRAW in one easy step, even if CorelDRAW is not running. Let's make some changes to our figure from Lesson 6.

1 Scroll through the window until you see the file labeled **lesson6.cdr**.

2 Double-click the thumbnail.

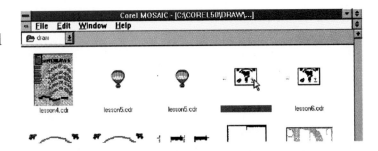

* CorelDRAW is launched and the file named **lesson6.cdr** is opened. Since you aren't going to be working in CorelDRAW right now, you can close it and return to Corel MOSAIC.

3 Double-click the **Close** box on the **CorelDRAW** window.

Double-click here

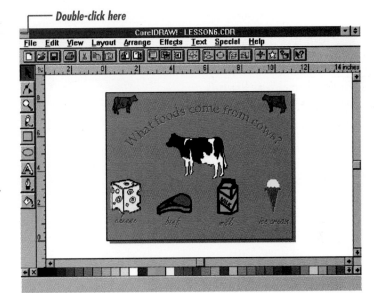

* The Mosaic window is exactly as it was before you launched CorelDRAW.

4 Double-click the **Close** box on the window containing your lesson files.

Now that you've located a file by browsing through a directory, you may find it quicker not to open a window of thumbnails right away. It may be easier to simply browse through thumbnails one at a time. Let's try to find the drawing you created with different types of text, assuming you might not be able to re-member the directory in which you saved it.

1 Open the File menu and choose Open Collection.

* The Open Collection dialog box is displayed.

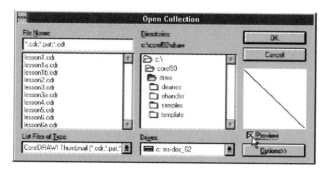

2 Select CorelDRAW! Thumb-nail in the List Files Of Type drop-down list.

3 Click in the Preview box if necessary to place a check in it.

4 In the Directories list box, double-click the directory where you've been saving your drawing files.

5 Double-click lesson1.cdr in the File Name box.

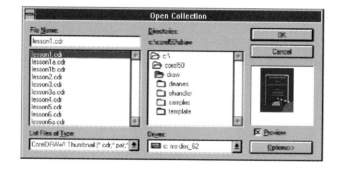

* The Preview window shows a thumbnail of that file.

6 Press ↓ to highlight the next file in the list, until you see the thumbnail you're looking for in the Preview window.

* When you do, you'll find that lesson4.cdr is highlighted in the File Name list box. Now that you've located the group of files, you can open a win-dow for them.

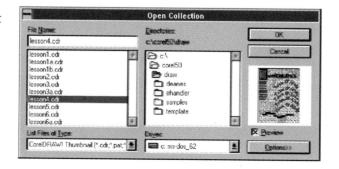

7 Click OK.

Creating a Catalog

You can organize drawings you create in CorelDRAW into a Corel MOSAIC *catalog*. A catalog is something you create and name to keep track of your files.

NOTE

A catalog doesn't change your file and directory structure; instead it's like a road map MOSAIC uses to display thumbnails, once you decide how you'd like them grouped.

To learn how to use a catalog, you'll create one for your lesson files.

✱ The window containing your lesson files is still open.

1 Open the **File** menu and choose **New Collection**.

✱ The Create New Collection dialog box is displayed.

2 Select **Corel Catalog (*.CLC)** in the **List Files Of Type** drop-down list.

3 Double-click the directory where you want to create the catalog. We chose **draw**.

4 Click in the **File Name** text box in front of the *, then press Del.

5 Type **lessons** as the catalog name.

6 Click in the **Description** text box and type a short description; for example, **quick & easy drawings**.

7 Click **OK**.

❊ The catalog is created as **lessons.clc** in the directory shown under **Directories**, and a new window is opened for that catalog.

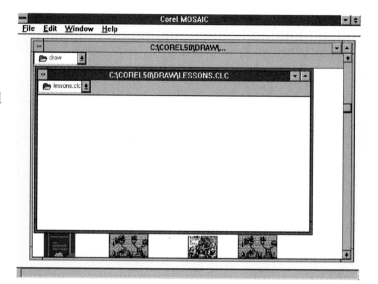

Once you create a catalog, you can put in it all the drawings which you've created during the lessons. This will be helpful if you saved them in different directories as you went along, and want to reorganize them. Since the Windows' drag-and-drop capability is part of Corel MOSAIC, placing drawings in a catalog is simple.

1 Open the **Window** menu and choose either **Tile Vertically** or **Tile Horizontally**.

❊ The figure shows the windows tiled vertically.

2 Place the mouse pointer on the thumbnail labeled **lesson1.cdr** and drag it to the empty window for the catalog **lessons.clc**.

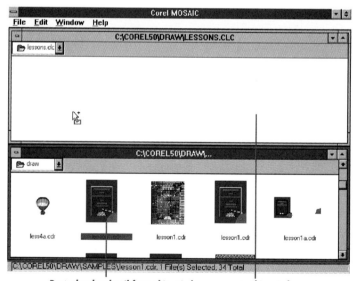

Drag the thumbnail from this window...   ...to this window

❊ You'll see a Copy Confirmation dialog box.

3 Choose **Yes**.

4 Click the thumbnail of **lesson2.cdr**.

5 Press and hold Ctrl, then click **lesson3.cdr, lesson4.cdr, lesson5.cdr**, and **lesson6.cdr**.

* All the lesson files are selected.

6 Place the mouse pointer on any one of the selected thumbnails and drag it to the window for the catalog **lessons.clc**.

* You'll see a Copy Confirmation dialog box.

7 Choose **Yes To All**.

* All the lesson files are added to the catalog. You now have one location for all your lesson files, and only your lesson files are stored there.

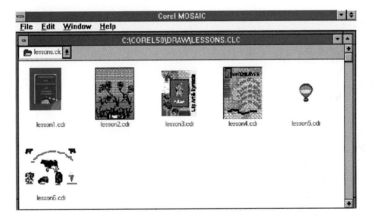

Adding Keywords

Another way you can categorize your files is by attaching words or short descriptions to them. These descriptions are called *keywords*, and you use a dialog box to attach them to files. Once you add keywords to files, you can always search through directories to find them.

Begin by closing the catalog—you won't be needing it just now. Double-click the **Close** box on the window titled **lessons.clc**.

Now add some keywords to the lesson files.

1 Click the thumbnail of **lesson1.cdr** in the Directory window to select it. All the other files are deselected.

2 Open the **Edit** menu and choose **Keywords**.

✳ The Keywords dialog box is displayed. The cursor is in the New Keyword text box.

3 Type the word **practice**.

4 Click **Add**.

✳ The word *practice* is added as a keyword.

5 Choose **Done**.

The keyword is added. However, there is a more efficient way to attach keywords to all your related files at once.

✳ **lesson1.cdr** is still selected.

1 Press and hold Ctrl, then click **lesson2.cdr**, **lesson3.cdr**, **lesson4.cdr**, **lesson5.cdr**, and **lesson6.cdr** to select the rest of your files.

2 Open the **Edit** menu and choose **Keywords** from the drop-down menu.

✱ The Keywords dialog box is opened.

3 Click on the word **practice** in the **Current Keywords** list box to select it.

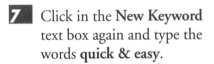

4 Click **Delete**.

5 Click in the **New Keyword** text box and type the word **lesson**.

6 Click **Add**.

7 Click in the **New Keyword** text box again and type the words **quick & easy**.

8 Click **Add**.

9 Click **Update All Selected Files** to place a check in the checkbox.

10 Click **Done**.

✳ You'll see a warning message.

11 Click **Yes**.

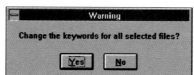

✳ All the selected files now have the same keywords: **lessons** and **quick & easy**.

Using Keywords to Find Files

Let's see how useful keywords are. They are helpful when you search through CorelDRAW's clip art files for a piece art to fit a particular need. Let's assume you are creating a design that requires weather pictures where people are included. We can use keywords to see what's available.

First, close the currently open catalog and directory windows by double-clicking the **Close** box on each window. You are going to search through one of CorelDRAW's clip art directories without opening the thumbnails.

1 Open the **File** menu and choose **Open Collection**.

✳ The Open Collection dialog box is displayed.

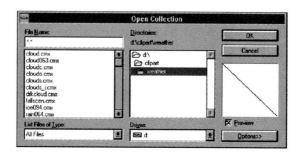

2 Select **All Image Files** in the **List Files Of Type** drop-down list.

3 In the **Directories** list box, double-click the **clipart** directory, then click **weather**.

4 Click **Options**.

✱ Additional options are displayed at the bottom of the dialog box.

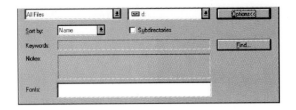

5 Click **Find**.

✱ The Keyword Search dialog box is displayed.

6 Type the word **woman**.

7 Open the **And** drop-down list on the next line down and click **Or**.

8 Click the text box to the right and type the word **man**.

9 Click below and type the word **snowman**.

10 Click **Start Search**.

✱ Corel MOSAIC searches the directory and displays in a new window all the clip art items that have *woman, man,* or *snowman* as keywords.

NOTE

You could also search through all CorelDRAW's clip art directories at once when looking for specific files or clip art. Just highlight the corel50 directory in the Directories list box and click the Subdirectories checkbox to place a check in it. However, be aware that it will take time to search through all of CorelDRAW's 40,000-plus clip art images.

Close this window before you go on to the next section by double-clicking the **Close** box on the window.

Printing Thumbnails

Sometimes when you have a collection of items, you'll want to print the thumbnails in that collection. By printing thumbnails, you can show the figures to others and have a record of them without using an excess of paper or time. To print thumbnails of your lesson drawings, begin by opening the catalog you created for them.

1 Open the File menu and choose **Open Collection**.

✱ The Open Collection dialog box is displayed.

2 Select **Corel Catalog File (*.CLC)** in the **List Files Of Type** drop-down list.

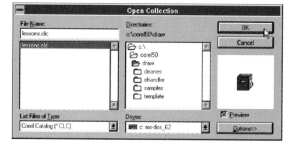

3 Double-click the directory where you created the catalog. We chose **draw**.

4 Click **lessons.clc** in the **File Names** list box.

5 Click **OK**.

✱ The catalog is opened in a new window.

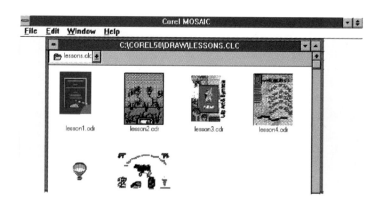

Setting Print Preferences

Printing thumbnails is similar to printing an individual drawing in CorelDRAW. You could select one or more items in this window and print them, or print all the displayed thumbnails.

To print all the thumbnails, you'll first want to set up the page for printing.

1 Open the **File** menu and choose **Preferences**.

✳ The Preferences dialog box opens. This is where you'll determine how large the thumbnails will be printed.

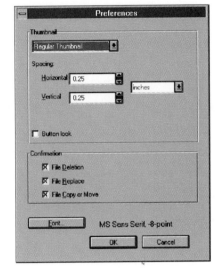

2 Choose **Regular Thumbnail** from the drop-down list to print the maximum number of thumbnails on the page.

3 Choose **OK**.

You are ready to print.

1 Open the **File** menu and choose **Print Thumbnails**.

✳ The Print dialog box is displayed and All is selected.

2 Click the **Options** button.

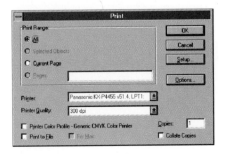

✱ The Print Options dialog box is displayed.

3 Click the **Options** tab.

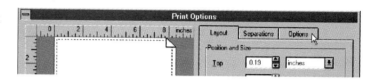

4 Click the **Print File Name** and **With Extension** check boxes to place a check in each.

5 Click **Header**.

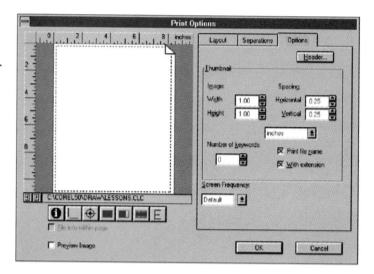

✱ The Header dialog box opens.

6 Check any items you'd like to see printed with the thumbnails; these will help you keep track of your files.

7 Click **Custom Text**.

8 Click in the text box and type **quick & easy lessons**.

9 Click **OK** in each of the three open dialog boxes (for a total of three times) to close all the dialog boxes and begin printing.

* All the thumbnails in the current window are printed.

Finishing Touches

Corel MOSAIC does not have the abundance of features that CorelDRAW has, but it is pretty handy when you're trying to find files and you can't remember what you named them. It is also the key to Corel's enormous clip art collection. If you have time, practice using the Keyword Search in a few directories, and create another catalog.

1 When you are finished, open the **File** menu and choose **Exit** to close Corel MOSAIC.

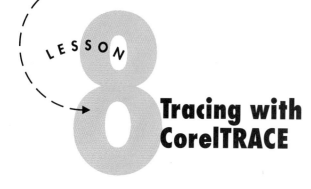

Tracing with CorelTRACE

20 MINUTES

In this lesson, you'll learn the basics of CorelTRACE while tracing different types of images. You'll also see how to trace an image and bring the traced image into CorelDRAW. CorelTRACE is handy for tracing scanned images, but since you may not have access to one, we used bitmap files (.pcx) from the **corel50\photopnt\samples** and **corel50\photopnt\tiles** directories.

Getting Started

The Corel5 group window contains the program icons that start the Corel applications. This is the same window from which you launched CorelDRAW.

Before you begin, double-click the **Corel5** icon at the bottom of the **Program Manager** window if the **Corel5** group window is not already open.

1 To start CorelTRACE, double-click the **CorelTrace** icon in the Corel5 group window.

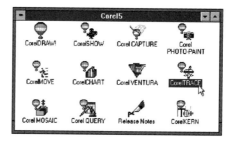

✳ The CorelTRACE window opens.

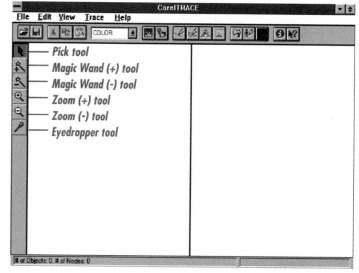

— Pick tool
— Magic Wand (+) tool
— Magic Wand (-) tool
— Zoom (+) tool
— Zoom (-) tool
— Eyedropper tool

NOTE

The window does not contain as many tools down the left side as CorelDRAW's main window does. And, there are fewer menus and other window components to learn before you get started.

Tracing an Image

Begin by tracing a file included in the **samples** directory.

1 Open the **File** menu and choose **Open**.

✱ The Open dialog box is displayed.

2 In the **List Files Of Type** box, select **Paintbrush (*.pcx)**.

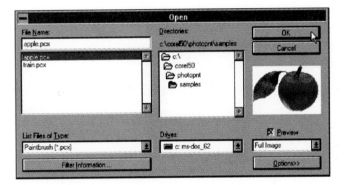

3 In the **Directories** list box, double-click **corel50**, double-click **photopnt**, then double-click **samples**.

4 In the **File Name** list box, click **apple.pcx**.(You may have to change to the CD-ROM drive to find this.)

5 Check the **Preview** box.

✱ Each image you highlight in the list box will be shown in the Preview window. Use this button before you select a file to make sure you want to import the image.

6 Choose **OK**.

✱ The image is shown in the left side of the window.

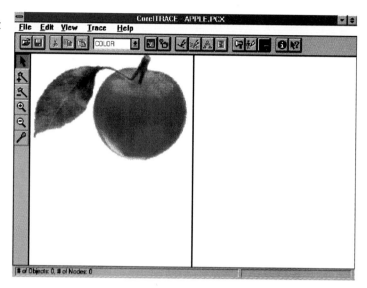

Choose the directory where you want the traced image stored. CorelTRACE doesn't prompt you to save the file after you trace an image—it stores it in the directory you've specified beforehand in the Save Options dialog box.

1 Open the File menu and choose Save Options.

✱ The Save Options dialog box is displayed.

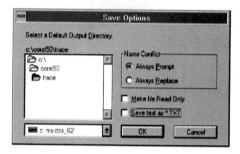

2 In the Directories list box, double-click corel50, then double-click trace.

3 Under Name Conflict, select Always Prompt.

✱ This will prevent Corel-TRACE from accidentally overwriting a previously-traced file that has the same file name.

4 Choose OK.

Now you'll try two tracing techniques, to see how they differ.

1 Open the Trace menu and choose **Woodcut**.

✱ The Woodcut method results in an image with lines across it at an angle.

2 Open the **Edit** menu and choose **Undo**.

3 Open the Trace menu and choose **Outline**.

Statistics for traced image are shown here

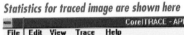

✱ The Outline method results in the edge of the image being traced and then filled in with a color similar to that in the source image.

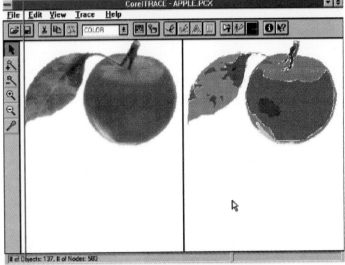

NOTE

Depending on your computer's processor speed and available memory, tracing may take a few minutes. You'll see an hourglass cursor and the percent completed, with a visual representation of the percentage in the fill bar. Once tracing is completed, you'll see information about the number of objects and nodes in the traced image, at the lower-left corner.

Saving a Traced Image

Save the traced image. Then we'll bring it into CorelDRAW for editing.

1 Open the **File** menu and choose **Save**, then choose **Trace As**.

✳ The **Save Trace As** dialog box is displayed.

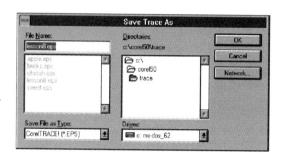

2 In the **Directories** list box, double-click **corel50**, then double-click **trace**.

3 Click in the **File Name** text box, then replace *.**eps** with **lesson8.eps** by deleting the * and typing **lesson8**.

4 Choose **OK**.

Modifying a Traced Image

There are two easy ways to modify a traced image. You can either import the image into CorelDRAW and modify it, or edit it in Corel PHOTO-PAINT. This section shows you how to bring the image into each application.

Importing a Traced Image into CorelDRAW

It's a simple process to minimize CorelTRACE, start CorelDRAW, and work with the traced image.

1 Click the minimize button at the upper-right corner of the window.

✱ The CorelTRACE icon is shown at the bottom of your screen.

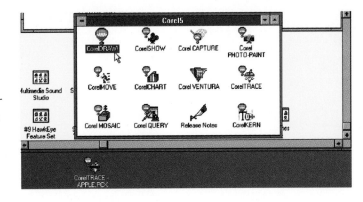

2 To start **CorelDRAW**, double-click the **CorelDRAW** icon in the **Corel5** group window.

3 Open the **File** menu and choose **Import**.

✱ The Import dialog box is displayed.

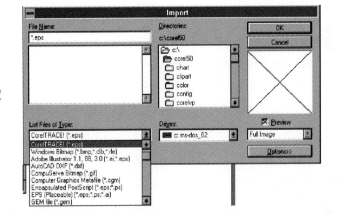

4 Open the **List Files Of Type** box and select **CorelTRACE!** (*.eps).

5 In the **Directories** list box, double-click **corel50**, then double-click **trace**.

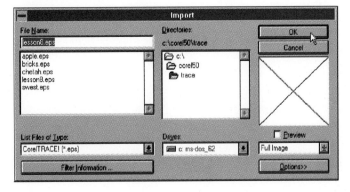

6 In the **File Name** list box, click **lesson8.eps**.

7 Click **OK**.

✳ You'll see a dialog box that tells you CorelDRAW is importing the file, then the file is displayed. You can work with it as you do any other image.

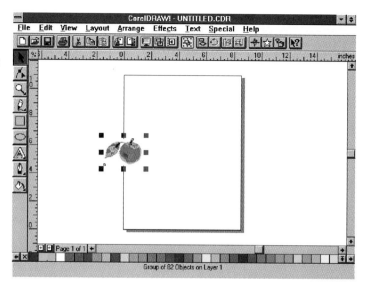

Modifying a Traced Image with CorelDRAW

Here's an example of how you'd modify part of a traced image. You'll notice in the status line that the image is a group of objects on one layer. Since we want to modify individual parts of the image, let's first ungroup it.

✳ The Pick tool is active.

1 Drag the image to your page.

2 Open the Arrange menu and choose Ungroup.

NOTE

You can drag a sizing handle to enlarge the picture; this is not necessary, just convenient.

3 Click outside the page, then click the leaf.

✳ The leaf is surrounded by a selection box.

4 Select a color in the color palette.

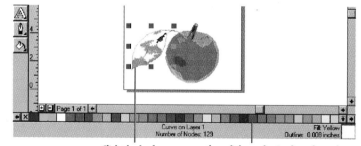

Click the leaf...   ...then click a color in the color palette

124

The leaf is filled with the color you selected, but no other part of the picture is changed. Try making some other modifications, using some of the techniques you learned in Lessons 1 through 6. You can work with a traced image in exactly the same way as other images, once it is imported into CorelDRAW. This is a good time to save your file.

1 Open the **File** menu and choose **Save**.

* The Save Drawing dialog box opens.

2 In the **File Name** box, type **lesson8.cdr**.

3 Choose **OK**.

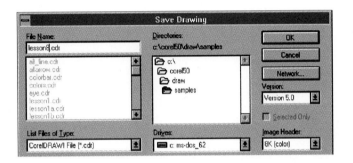

Printing a Traced Image

Let's print the image. You cannot print a traced image from CorelTRACE. To print, you'll import the file to CorelDRAW and print it from there.

1 Open the **File** menu and choose **Print**.

* The Print dialog box is displayed.

2 To print the entire drawing page, select **All**.

3 Click **OK**.

* Your drawing begins printing. Once it is finished, you are ready to exit CorelDRAW.

4   Open the **File** menu and
choose **Exit** to close **Corel-
DRAW** and return to the
Program Manager window.

Editing a Traced Image in Corel PHOTO-PAINT

Watch how easy it is to edit a traced image in Corel PHOTO-PAINT.
First, you'll reopen CorelTRACE.

1   Double-click the minimized
CorelTRACE program icon.

✳   CorelTRACE is re-activated.

2   Open the **Edit** menu and
choose **Edit Image**.

✳   The image is opened in Corel
PHOTO-PAINT and can be
edited here, as well. Corel
PHOTO-PAINT is covered in
the next lesson, so you may not
have the skills to edit a traced
image here yet. We'll go back to
CorelTRACE for now.

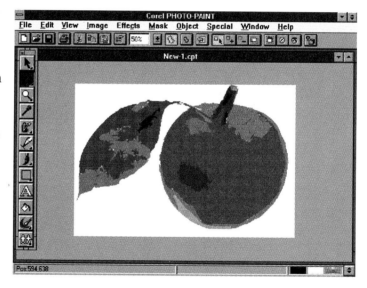

3   Open the **File** menu and
choose **Exit**.

✳ The CorelTRACE window is visible and the image you traced is still in the Tracing window.

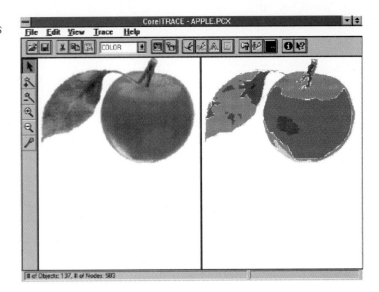

More Tracing Techniques

There are two other handy techniques you may want to use:

- Selecting and tracing part of an image

- Selecting and tracing several images

Tracing Part of an Image

There are going to be times when you need to trace a part of an image instead of a complete image. CorelTRACE provides two different tools to help you. First, we'll use the Magic Wand tool.

1 Open the **Edit** menu and choose **Clear** to remove the traced image from the window.

2 Click the **Magic Wand** (+) tool.

NOTE

The Magic Wand (+) tool lets you select an area of any shape and similar color to the area you click.

3 Click on the leaf of the apple.

✱ You'll see a marquee (which selects an irregularly shaped area for tracing) marking the selection. The marquee appears as a moving black and white line around the leaf.

Marquee

4 Open the Trace menu and choose Outline.

✱ You'll see the partial outline trace in the window at the right.

Tracing Several Parts of an Image

Now trace several parts of the image using the Silhouette method.

1 Open the Edit menu and choose Clear to remove the traced image from the window.

✱ The Magic Wand (+) tool is still active.

2 Click on the outline of the apple.

✱ Only part of the apple is selected, because the entire apple is not the same shade of red.

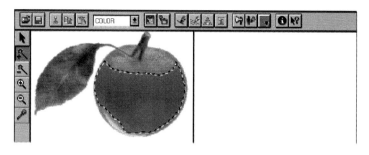

3 Press Shift and click on another area of the apple that is not yet selected. Continue pressing Shift and clicking until you have most of the apple selected.

Marquee

4 Click the **Color** button in the ribbon bar and choose a color for the traced image.

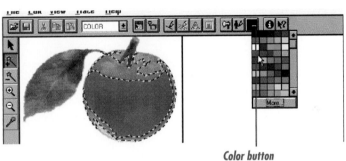

Color button

5 Open the **Trace** menu and choose **Silhouette**.

✳ You'll see the partial silhouette in the window at the right, in the color you chose.

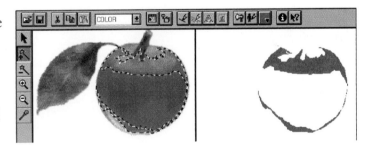

6 Go back to the apple and click any additional areas you missed in your first trace. You can add these to the existing trace.

7 Open the **Trace** menu and choose **Silhouette**.

✳ You'll see the partial silhouette in the window at the right.

Now trace the stem of the apple in a different color.

✳ The Magic Wand (+) tool is still active.

1 Click on the stem of the apple.

2 Continue pressing Shift and clicking until you have most of the stem selected.

Marquee

3 Click the **Color** button and choose a different color for the traced image of the apple stem. (Scroll the color palette to reveal additional colors.)

Color button

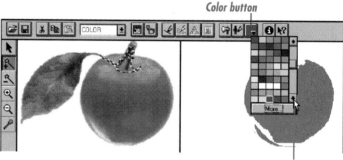

Press here to display additional colors

4 Open the **Trace** menu and choose **Silhouette**.

✳ You'll see the built-up silhou-ette in the window at the right, which is a result of the multiple traces you've just done.

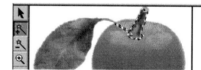

You can use the Pick tool as you do in CorelDRAW to draw a marquee selec-tion box around part of an image in order to select only part of it for tracing. Begin by removing the traced image from the window.

1 Open the **Edit** menu and choose **Clear**.

2 Click the **Pick** tool.

3 Start at the upper-left corner of the apple and drag the cursor to the lower-right corner, then release the mouse button.

Selection box

✳ The apple is selected without the leaf.

4 Open the Trace menu and choose Outline.

✳ The outline of the partial image you selected is traced and then displayed in the Tracing window.

Tracing Multiple Images

Try selecting and tracing several images at one time.

1 Open the File menu and choose Open.

2 Click No when you see the message Save current trace?

✳ The Open Files dialog box is displayed.

3 In the Directories list box, double-click corel50, double-click photopnt, then double-click tiles.

4 In the **List Files Of Type** box, select **Paintbrush (*.pcx)**.

5 In the **File Name** list box, click **bricks.pcx**.

6 Check the **Preview** box.

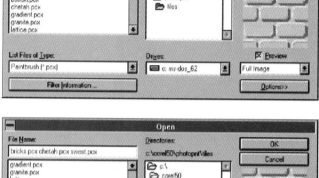

7 In the **File Name** list box, press C trl and click **cheetah.pcx**, then C trl+click **swest.pcx**.

✱ If there are any other files you'd like to try tracing, select them by C trl+clicking each. All your selections will be high-lighted in the list box and the name of each selected image is added to the File Name text box.

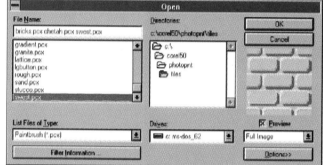

8 Choose **OK**.

✱ The Batch File roll-up is opened, with the names of the three files displayed. You can now trace the files as a group.

9 In the **Batch File** roll-up, click **Trace All**.

CorelTRACE traces each image, one at a time. Information about each is shown in the bottom of the window. The files are saved with an **.eps** exten-sion in the directory you specified earlier in this lesson. Once all the images are traced, the window is blank.

When you've finished tracing, close the roll-up by double-clicking the **Close** box.

Setting Tracing Options

Let's try setting the Tracing Options differently for one image. The Tracing Options are initially set to provide a balance between the best possible trace and a reasonable amount of resulting time and disk space. If the default settings do not produce the result you want, you can adjust the options until you are satisfied.

1 Open the **File** menu and choose **Open**.

2 In the **Directories** list box, double-click **corel50**, double-click **photopnt**, then double-click **tiles**.

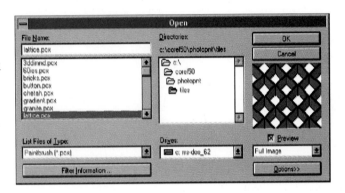

3 In the **List Files Of Type** box, select **Paintbrush (*.pcx)**.

4 In the **File Name** list box, click **lattice.pcx**.

5 Choose **OK**.

✳ The file is displayed on the left side of the window.

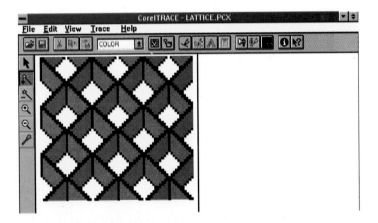

NOTE

If you've used CorelTRACE previously and changed any of the default options, the file may display differently in this window.

6 Open the Trace menu and choose **Outline**.

❋ The result is shown in the window on the right.

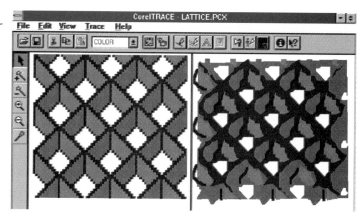

Now change several tracing options and trace the image again.

1 Open the Trace menu and choose **Edit Options**.

❋ The Tracing Options dialog box is displayed.

2 Check **Smooth Dithering**. (This causes CorelTRACE to smooth pixels to improve the image.)

3 Click the **Lines** tab.

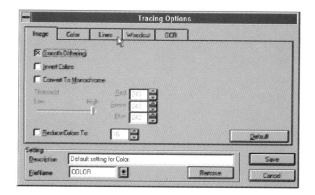

4 Select **Very Good** from the **Curve Precision** drop-down list.

5 Select **Very Good** from the **Line Precision** drop-down list.

6 Select **Very Short** from the **Target Curve Length** drop-down list.

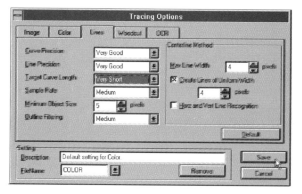

7 Click **Save**.

8 Open the **Trace** menu and choose **Outline**.

✳ The result is shown in the window on the right.

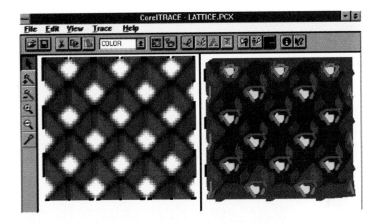

NOTE

If you are not satisfied with either of these images, try experimenting with the options in the Tracing Options dialog box. The on-line Help provides a description of each option.

Finishing Touches

Once you trace an image, you can enhance it in CorelDRAW or edit it in Corel PHOTO-PAINT. You may find this enhancement capability the best reason for using CorelTRACE. So, before going on to Lesson 9, select one of the images you traced to import into CorelDRAW and enhance it, to see if you agree.

1 When you are finished, open the **File** menu and choose **Exit** to close **CorelTRACE**.

9 Touching Up Photos with Corel PHOTO-PAINT

30 MINUTES

This lesson provides you with the opportunity to try some of Corel PHOTO-PAINT's retouching tools to clean up, enhance, and otherwise modify a scanned image. However, you can try out the tools even if you don't have a scanned image by doing either of the following:

- Open any .TIF file. Some are included in the **clipart\ _bitmaps\old_west** directory on the CD-ROM.

- If you have purchased CorelDRAW on CD-ROM, use one of the sample photos included on the CD-ROMs.

Although you won't have an identical image to the one you see here, you'll be able to use the tools for similar areas in your image. We recommend you use a color image, so you'll be able to see the effect of the color tools.

Getting Started

1 Double-click the **Corel PHOTO-PAINT** icon in the **Corel5** group window.

✳ The Corel PHOTO-PAINT window is opened.

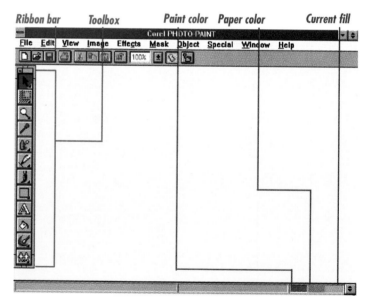

NOTE

The main items in the window, besides the standard Windows elements, are the button bar and Toolbox. The Toolbox has more tools than the one in CorelDRAW. You'll also open several roll-ups, which you'll want to keep open most of the time.

Opening an Image

Let's start working on the file you've scanned or selected.

1 Open the **File** menu and choose **Open**.

✱ The Open An Image dialog box is displayed.

2 Open the **List Files Of Type** dialog box and select **TIFF Bitmap** (*.tif, *.jtf, *.sep).

✱ To edit a PCX file, choose **Paintbrush** (*.pcx) instead.

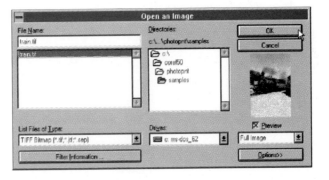

3 In the **Directories** list box, double-click the directory where the file is located.

4 Click the file name in the **File Name** list box.

5 Click **OK**.

✱ The picture you selected is displayed. The example we've selected is a scanned photograph of a train, in TIF format.

Matching and Modifying Colors

The first change we'll make is to the sky, changing the color of the sky to match one of the existing colors.

> **NOTE**
>
> Corel PHOTO-PAINT lets you specify two colors, which are referred to as the *paint* color and the *paper* color. You can also specify a fill for objects, called the *current fill*, which can be a solid color, pattern, or texture. This lesson lets you practice setting and changing colors and fills that are used with different tools.

1 Open the View menu and choose **Color Roll-Up**.

✴ You may want to drag the roll-up to the side so it will be out of your way.

2 Click the **Eyedropper** tool.

3 Press Ctrl and click with the eyedropper in the area of the picture containing the color you want to match.

✴ The color you chose becomes the paper color. It is placed in the Color roll-up and also is displayed in the lower-right corner of the window. You can use the paper color to erase the background and replace the color at the same time.

Eyedropper tool   *Click the color to match*   *Paper color shows here*

4 Click the Local Undo tool, then click the Eraser tool in the flyout.

Local Undo tool   Eraser tool

* The Eraser tool uses the paper color to replace the background color.

5 Open the View menu and choose the Tool Settings roll-up (and then drag it to the side).

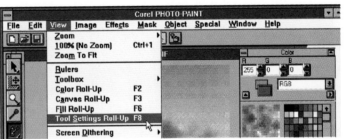

* You can change the brush width and size in the Tool Settings roll-up to achieve different effects.

6 Click the square brush shape.

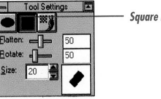

Square brush shape

7 Drag the Flatten control to the right to decrease the brush height until it reaches 50, or type 50 in the text box.

8 Drag the Rotate control to the right to turn the brush on an angle until it reaches 50, or type 50 in the text box.

9 Type 20 for the brush Size.

10 Drag the Eraser back and forth over the area to cover it with the color.

* The Eraser's path is filled with the paper color. Try moving the mouse more slowly than usual, for a more satisfying result.

Drag the Eraser back and forth

NOTE

To fill in the larger areas, use a large brush size. For the finer areas, you'll want to flatten and probably rotate the brush for better accuracy.

Zooming In

You'll probably want to magnify this area so you can work on more detail. In fact, it's usually helpful to magnify part of your image.

NOTE

The Zoom tool in Corel PHOTO-PAINT works differently from the Zoom tool in CorelDRAW, as you can only zoom in and out at fixed increments.

1 Click the Zoom tool.

2 Point to the area you want to magnify and click the left mouse button.

✳ Clicking the left mouse button magnifies the picture to 200% and shows you the area you selected. Since the area still may not be magnified enough, try the next step.

3 Point to the area and click again.

✳ Clicking again magnifies the area by another 100% (to 300%).

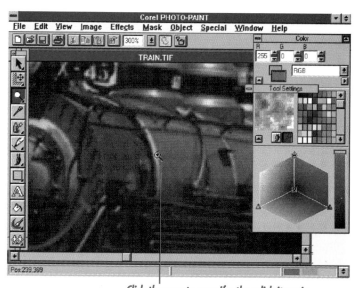

Click the area to magnify, then click it again

To return to Normal view at any time later:

1 Right-click with the **Zoom** tool.

* Right-clicking reduces the size of the area by 100%.

Or, you can choose a magnification level for the entire image from the Zoom drop-down list in the ribbon bar.

1 Choose **300%** from the **Zoom** drop-down list to try working in magnified view.

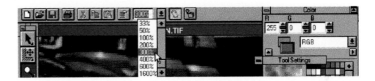

Enhancing Detail

We'll add some detail to the train, by adding the gold color to the color palette and then using the Pen to enhance the detail.

1 Click the **Eyedropper** tool.

2 Click the color you want to match.

* The color is placed in the Color roll-up and becomes the new paint color.

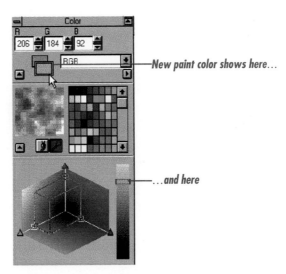

New paint color shows here...

...and here

3 Click and hold on the **Line** tool, then click on the **Pen** tool in the flyout.

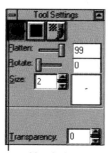

Line tool   *Pen tool*

4 In the **Tool Settings** roll-up, click the round brush shape.

5 Drag the **Flatten** control to the right to increase the height of the brush to **99**.

6 Drag the **Rotate** control to the left so the brush is not on an angle and has a value of **0**.

Round brush shape

7 Type **2** for the **Size** of the brush.

NOTE

Different options are displayed in the Tool Settings roll-up as you change tools.

8 Type **0** in the **Transparency** text box.

9 Enhance the detail to make it crisper and more distinct by dragging the pen back and forth over the existing detail.

Drag the Pen tool over existing detail

Spraying Colors

Next, we selected four different colors and blended them to give the ground the look of dried grass. Apply this technique to an area of your picture where you'd like a more textured look.

1 Click the **Eyedropper** on a color to make it the paint color.

2 Click and hold on the **Paintbrush** tool, then click the **Spraycan** tool on the flyout.

Paintbrush tool   *Spraycan tool*

3 In the **Tool Settings** roll-up, click the square brush shape.

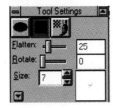

4 Drag the **Flatten** control to the left to increase the height of the brush so it has a value of **25**, or type **25** in the text box.

5 Type 7 for the **Size** of the brush.

6 Drag the **Spraycan** back and forth to splatter an area with paint.

Drag the Spraycan back and forth

Repeat the following steps three times to get three additional colors:

1 Click the **Eyedropper** on a color to make it the paint color.

2 Click the **Spraycan** tool.

3 Drag the **Spraycan** back and forth to splatter an area with paint.

Blending Colors

When you have all four colors painted in, you can blend them together.

1 Click the **Smear** tool, then click the **Blend** tool on the flyout.

Smear tool   Blend tool

2 In the **Tool Settings** roll-up, click the square brush shape.

3 Drag the **Flatten** control further to the left to decrease the height of the brush to a value of **10**, or type **10** in the text box.

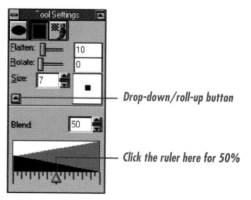

Drop-down/roll-up button

Click the ruler here for 50%

4 Click the drop-down button in the roll-up if necessary to open it.

5 Set the degree of blend to 50% by clicking or dragging on the ruler or typing **50** in the text box.

6 Drag the **Blend** tool back and forth over the area you want to blend.

Retouching with Tools

Corel PHOTO-PAINT includes both retouch tools and filters that improve the appearance of the image. Some are applied to a limited area or object, while others are applied to the entire image. First, use the retouch tools to improve specific objects.

1 Click and hold on the **Blend** tool, then click the **Sharpen** tool on the flyout.

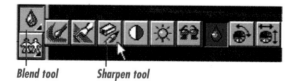

Blend tool   Sharpen tool

2 In the **Tool Settings** roll-up, set the degree of sharpening to 75% by clicking on the ruler or typing **75** in the text box.

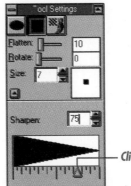

Click the ruler here for 75%

3 Drag the **Sharpen** tool back and forth over an area that seems blurred.

✳ We sharpened the train's number.

Drag the Sharpen tool over a blurred area

Lightening an Image

You can also lighten part of your image.

1 Click the **Sharpen** tool, then click the **Brightness** tool on the flyout.

✳ You do not have to change the brush settings.

Sharpen tool   *Brightness tool*

2 Drag the tool over an area that you'd like to lighten.

✳ We lightened the engineer.

Drag the Brightness tool over a dark area

Sharpening an Image

Now we'll try some filters and apply them to the whole image. For these steps, you'll want to return to 100% magnification to see the whole image.

1 To return to **Normal** view, choose **100%** from the **Zoom** drop-down list on the button bar.

2 Open the **Effects** menu and choose **Sharpen**, then choose **Sharpen** again from the cascading menu.

✳ The Sharpen dialog box is displayed.

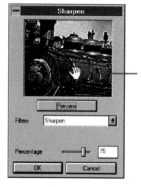

3 Select a value of 75% by clicking on the ruler or typing 75 in the text box to sharpen the image that much.

Drag the image around in the Preview box

4 Click **Preview** to see how the image will change.

5 Hold down the left mouse button and use the hand cursor to drag the image around in the **Preview** box. This will let you pan the entire image in the box.

NOTE

When you use Preview, the change is only applied to the portion of the image that is displayed. This speeds up the preview process.

6 Click **OK**.

✳ The entire image is sharpened, especially the edges, and detailed areas are enhanced.

Improving Brightness and Contrast

You can also enhance the brightness and contrast of an image.

1 Open the **Effects** menu again and choose **Color**, then choose **Brightness and Contrast** from the cascading menu.

✱ The Brightness-Contrast-Intensity dialog box is displayed.

2 Set the **Brightness** to 15, set the **Contrast** to 5, and set the **Intensity** to 8.

3 Click **Preview** to see how the image will change.

4 Hold down the left mouse button and use the hand cursor to drag the image around in the Preview box.

5 Change the settings and select Preview again.

6 When you are satisfied with results of the settings, choose **OK**.

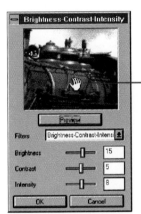

Drag the image around in the Preview box

NOTE

Every image requires different settings in this dialog box to achieve a desired result. Remember, image enhancement is an art, not a science.

Copying and Pasting

It's as easy to duplicate a rectangular object in Corel PHOTO-PAINT as it is in CorelDRAW. We wanted to remove the car and house at the left of the picture and paste some additional trees there. That can be accomplished by copying and pasting small parts of the trees.

1 Click and hold on the **Mask Picker** tool, then click the **Rectangle Mask** tool on the flyout.

Mask Picker tool   Rectangular Mask tool

2 Select part of a tree (or any object in your image) by dragging the pointer from the top left to the bottom right of the area and releasing the mouse button.

Drag from here...   ...to here

✻ The area is surrounded by a rectangle.

NOTE
The dotted lines around the selected areas are removed once you save the image.

3 Open the **Edit** menu and choose **Copy**.

4 Open the **Edit** menu again and choose **Paste**, then choose **As New Object**.

✻ The area is pasted to the center of the window and is selected.

5 Drag the area to the front of the car (or the object you want to replace).

Drag the pasted object to here...   ...from here

6 Drag any corner to decrease or increase the size of the trees slightly.

7 Repeat steps 4–6 several times, until the area is covered.

NOTE
Remember, as in CorelDRAW, you can drag the Toolbox around on the screen whenever you need to move it out of your way.

Blending Objects

Because the trees should be blended together and not stand out, you can use additional techniques that will result in a better image. You'll want to zoom in to the area you will be working on before you begin.

1 Click the **Zoom** tool.

2 Point to the area you want to magnify and click the left mouse button. Then click the same area again.

Now you are ready to try some blending techniques.

1 Click the **Eyedropper** tool.

2 Click one of the colors in the tree to make it the paint color.

3 Click the **Spraycan** tool.

4 Drag the tool over the edges that resulted when you pasted a rectangular selection.

5 Repeat steps 1, 2, and 3 for several additional colors in the tree.

Drag the tool over the edges

Now that you have several colors sprayed in, you can smudge them.

1 Click and hold on the **Brightness** tool, then click the **Smudge** tool on the flyout.

Brightness tool   Smudge tool

2 In the **Tool Settings** roll-up, choose **Soft** from the **Edge** drop-down list.

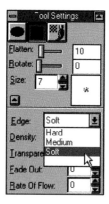

3 Drag the tool back and forth over the sharp edges to soften them.

Instead of clearly defined objects, you now have a group of objects blended together. Try using both the Smear and Smudge tools to see the difference in the results.

Undoing Mistakes

Corel PHOTO-PAINT's Undo command only reverses the last edit or stroke that you made. For example, if you are unhappy with the effect you just created with the Freehand Smudge tool, do the following:

1 Open the **Edit** menu and choose **Undo Brush Stroke**.

✳ You'll notice that only the very last stroke was reversed.

2 Click the **Local Undo** tool.

3 Drag it back and forth across the last area on which you worked.

✳ You'll notice you can reverse the effects in that area.

NOTE

You can also use the Local Undo tool to reverse previous actions.

4 Drag it back and forth across an area you worked on earlier.

✳ You'll notice you can no longer reverse the effects in that area.

Corel PHOTO-PAINT does offer you a way to reverse previous actions, with the Checkpoint/Restore To Checkpoint commands. But you'll have to think ahead in order to be able to use them. You'll want to choose Checkpoint every few minutes in order to save a working copy of your image. Then, when you've made a change to your document which you aren't happy with, you can return to that image with the Restore To Checkpoint command.

NOTE

Checkpoint saves a copy of your image to computer memory, but does not save a copy on the hard disk. You'll need to use the Save command, described later in this lesson, to save a permanent copy on the hard disk.

Establish a checkpoint now:

1 Open the **Edit** menu and choose **Checkpoint**.

✳ We'll remind you to use **Restore To Checkpoint** later.

Creating Objects

You may have noticed that there are some blank areas in your image that need more than color—they need objects. We'll draw an ellipse with the Circle tool at the bottom right of the image, then add a label for the image. First, return to Normal view:

1 Choose **100%** from the **Zoom** drop-down list on the ribbon bar.

✱ You can see the entire image and place the shape properly.

2 Click and hold on the **Rectangle** tool, then click the **Ellipse** tool on the flyout.

— *Rectangle tool*
— *Ellipse tool*

✱ You do not have to change the tool settings.

3 Position the cursor near the bottom of the page, press the left mouse button, and drag the mouse until you make an ellipse about three inches wide, then release the mouse button.

Drag the cursor from here...   ...to here

✱ When you release the mouse button, the ellipse is filled with the current fill and out-lined in the paint color.

You can change the color of the ellipse with the Fill tool before you go on.

1 Open the **View** menu and choose **Fill Roll-Up**.

✱ The Fill roll-up is opened.

2 Click the **Color** button to open the color palette.

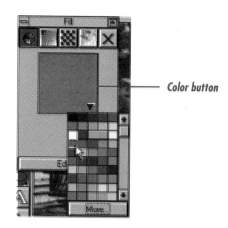

— *Color button*

3 Click a new color in the palette.

✱ This selects the current fill.

4 Click the **Fill** tool.

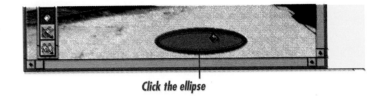

5 Click inside the ellipse.

✳ The ellipse is filled with the new color.

Click the ellipse

The color combination isn't really what we had in mind, so we'll try this again.

1 Open the **Edit** menu and choose **Restore To Checkpoint**.

✳ PHOTO-PAINT replaces the image on the screen with the image you previously saved with the Checkpoint command.

CTL/F2

2 In the **Color** roll-up, click the front rectangle to define a new paint color.

3 Click a new color in the palette.

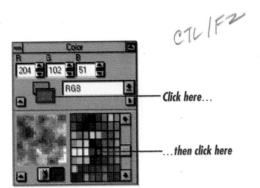

Click here...

...then click here

✳ The outline of the ellipse will be drawn in this color.

4 In the **Fill** roll-up, click the **Color** button to open the color palette.

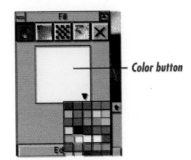

Color button

5 Click a new color in the palette.

* The ellipse will be filled with this color.

6 Click the **Ellipse** tool.

7 Draw an ellipse about three inches wide with the tool.

Now let's continue adding to the image.

Adding Text

Next you'll create a label within the ellipse.

1 Click the **Text** tool.

* Notice that additional tools are added to the ribbon bar.

2 Select a typeface from the drop-down list in the ribbon bar.

3 Select a point size from the drop-down list in the ribbon bar.

Select a typeface here   Select a point size here

4 Click in the left side of the ellipse to add text to it.

5 Type the words **Lesson 9**.

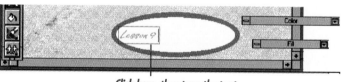

Click here, then type the text

* Notice that the text was added in the paint color.

6 Click the **Pick** tool to select the text you just typed.

7 Drag the selection box to place the text in the center of the ellipse.

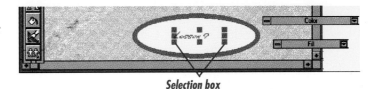

Selection box

Painting Lines

Add a line below the text to make it look more interesting. Before you work with the Line tool, set a new Checkpoint.

1 Open the **Edit** menu and choose **Checkpoint**.

2 Click the **Pen** tool, then click the **Line** tool in the flyout.

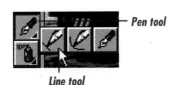

Pen tool

Line tool

3 In the **Tool Settings** roll-up, enter a 2 for the **Size** of the tool.

4 In the **Color** roll-up, click a new color in the palette to define the paint color.

5 Draw a zigzag line below the text by clicking at the line's starting point then clicking at each angle until the line is complete. Then double-click at the ending point.

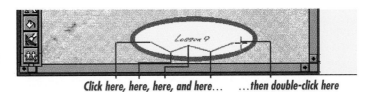

Click here, here, here, and here...   ...then double-click here

6 Since this doesn't look the way we want it to, open the **Edit** menu and choose **Restore To Checkpoint**.

7 Draw a straight line below the text by clicking at the line's starting point then double-clicking at the ending point.

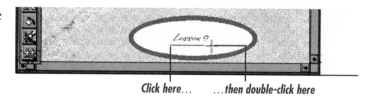

Click here...   ...then double-click here

Now you're ready to save your image.

Saving Your Image

To save your touched-up image and keep your original scan or image on disk intact, do the following:

1 Open the **File** menu and choose **Save As**.

* The Save An Image To Disk dialog box is displayed.

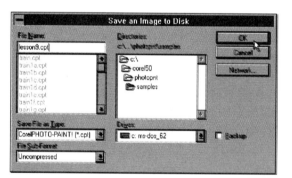

2 Open the **List Files Of Type** box and select **CorelPHOTO-PAINT (*.cpt)**.

3 Type **lesson9.cpt** in the **File Name** text box.

4 Select **Uncompressed** from the **File Sub-Format** drop-down list.

5 Click **OK**.

Printing Your Image

To print your image, do the following:

1 Open the **File** menu and choose **Print**.

✱ The Print dialog box is
    displayed.

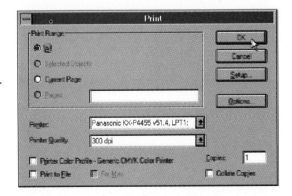

2 Under **Print Range**, select **All**.

3 Click **OK**.

✱ The Printing File dialog box is
    displayed and your painting
    is printed.

Finishing Touches

We used several of the tools from this lesson to add the following touches to
our image:

- We erased the train car on the right of the image using a sky-colored
  eraser.

- We copied and pasted parts of the ground to fill it in, and blended the
  two areas with the Smear Paintbrush tool.

- We copied and pasted the railroad tracks from the front of the train to
  the back, so the train wasn't coming out of the sky.

NOTE

Don't forget to use the Undo command on the Edit menu right after changes you
wish you hadn't made. Remember also to set your checkpoints at regular intervals
so that you can return to an earlier version of your image if you make a mistake
that you need to undo.

Try using all the tools and the filters to see how much they change, and hope-fully, improve the image. When you are finished trying things out, save and print your image.

Here's how our scanned image looked, after we finished adding our enhance-ments to it.

Appendix

Where Do I Go from Here?

In the course of reading and using this book, you've learned a great deal about CorelDRAW techniques and features, and have acquired basic skills with the Corel MOSAIC, CorelTRACE, and Corel PHOTO-PAINT applications. You have a firm grasp on the essentials, but since CorelDRAW is such a powerful program, you'll probably want to learn about its other capabilities at some point. For example, you might want to learn how to create artistic effects with CorelDRAW's new PowerClip feature. You also may want to learn to use Corel Ventura to desktop-publish your longer documents, or use CorelCHART to quickly turn your spreadsheet data into charts. Perhaps you need to create an animated show with CorelMOVE, or to develop a presentation with CorelSHOW.

If you think you're ready for a how-to book that doubles as a reference and covers all the CorelDRAW applications in depth, try *Mastering CorelDRAW 5, Special Edition*, by Rick Altman, SYBEX, 1994. It's full of great examples and hands-on exercises, and it explains everything from the most basic topics to the most advanced.

If you plan to use Corel Ventura, then move on to *Corel Ventura 5 Plain & Simple*, by Robin Merrin, SYBEX, 1994. It will help you learn all the essential features of Corel Ventura 5, using the same approach as this book—structured lessons supported by hundreds of illustrations.

Index

Symbols

% Of Char. Height, 63

A

Align button (ribbon bar), 100
aligning text and drawing, 99–100
application window, 2, 18
    Corel MOSAIC, 102
    Corel PHOTO-PAINT, 136
    CorelTRACE, 118
Arrange menu
    Break Apart, 42
    Group, 100
    Order, Back One, 44, 60
    Ungroup, 124
arranging objects, 41–44
arrow, mouse pointer as, 3
Artistic Text tool, 2, 11, 46, 50, 53, 94
attributes of text, copying, 96–97
AutoJoin feature, 23

B

background for text, 45, 49–50
Batch File roll-up, 132
Bezier tool, 22–23
    vs. Freehand tool, 20
Bitmap Export dialog box, 74
Blend tool, 144
blending
    colors, 21, 143–144
    objects, 149–150
boldface font style, 56
Break Apart (Arrange menu), 42

Brightness-Contrast-Intensity dialog box, 147
brightness of image, improving, 146–147
Brightness tool, 145, 149
brush, changing size in Corel PHOTO-PAINT, 139
buttons, 82
    information about, 83

C

catalogs, creating in Corel MOSAIC, 107–109
CD-ROM
    clip art and symbols on, 36, 37
    importing file from, 89
*.cdt file type, 75
Center Justification button (Text roll-up), 13, 56
Character Attributes dialog box, 57–58
Checkpoint, 151, 157
circles, 5–9
    text placement on, 52
Clear (Edit menu), 128
*.CLC file type, 107
clip art
    on CD-ROM, 36, 37
    importing, 36–38, 88–90
    rotating, 39
    searching directories, 113
Clipboard
    copying drawing to, 27
    copying with, 77–80
clone, color changes and, 44
Clone (Edit menu), 42
closing objects, 22
*.cmx file type, 89

CMYK Color Model, 86
color
blending, 143–144
changes and clones, 44
changing, 124–125
of outline, 46
spraying, 142–143
for symbols, 41
of text, 12, 31, 47, 97
for traced image, 129
Color button (Outline Pen dialog box), 11
color palette, 2, 4
in Corel PHOTO-PAINT, 152
scrolling, 28
Color roll-up, 141
column of text, selecting, 76–77
contrast of image, improving, 146–147
Control menu, Grouped, 19
Copy (Edit menu), 27, 79
Copy Attributes dialog box, 97
Copy Attributes From (Edit menu), 97
copying
attributes of text, 96–97
with Clipboard, 77–80
in Corel PHOTO-PAINT, 147–148
objects, 79–80
paragraph text, 78–79
Corel5 group window, 1
Corel MOSAIC
creating catalog, 107–109
keywords, 109–113
starting, 102
thumbnails in, 38–39, 103–106
Corel PHOTO-PAINT, 136–158
adding text, 154–155
blending objects, 149–150
color palette in, 152
copying and pasting, 147–148
editing traced image, 126–127
exporting file for, 74–75
Eyedropper tool, 141
Normal view in, 141
object creation, 151–154
printing in, 156–157

saving image, 156
Undo, 150–151
window, 136
zooming in, 140–141
Corel Presentation Exchange file type, 89
Corel Ventura, 72
CorelDRAW
exiting, 17
importing traced image into, 122–124
launching, 1
CorelTRACE, 118–135
icon, 123
modifying traced image, 122–125
setting options, 133–135
tracing, 119–121
tracing part of image, 127–128
window, 118
*.cpt file format, 156
Create New Collection dialog box, 107
crosshairs, mouse cursor as, 2, 3
Ctrl key
with Ellipse tool, 5
with Freehand tool, 15
with Rectangle tool, 5
current fill, in Corel PHOTO-PAINT, 136
Curve Precision drop-down list (Tracing Options dialog box), 134
curving text, 50–53
custom install, and symbols availability, 87

D

default settings
for fill, 85–86
for outlines, 84–85
Delete (Edit menu), 23
deleting
guidelines, 92–93
objects, 23
selected items, 77
directories
for saved drawing, 9
searching for clip art, 113
for traced image, 120

displaying
    grid, 98–99
    guidelines, 86–87
    rulers, 18
    tools, 19
dragging objects, and guidelines, 90
drawing page, 2
drawings
    aligning with text, 99–100
    copying to Clipboard, 27
    printing entire page, 16
    saving, 9
    starting new, 19–20
Drives drop-down list, 37
Duplicate (Edit menu), 3, 24, 41, 66, 91

E

Edit Image (Edit menu), 126
Edit menu
    Clone, 42
    Copy, 27, 79
    Copy Attributes From, 97
    Delete, 23
    Duplicate, 3, 24, 41, 66, 91
    Paste, 27, 79
    Repeat, 100
    Repeat Duplicate, 25
    Undo, 23, 121
    Undo Fill, 5
Edit menu (Corel MOSAIC), Keywords, 111
Edit menu (Corel PHOTO-PAINT)
    Checkpoint, 151
    Copy, 148
    Paste As New Object, 148
    Restore To Checkpoint command, 151, 153, 155
    Undo, 157
    Undo Brush Stroke, 150
Edit menu (CorelTRACE)
    Clear, 128
    Edit Image, 126

Edit Options (Trace menu), 134
Edit Text dialog box, 57
editing
    in Corel PHOTO-PAINT, 126–127
    page, 2
    text, 56–61
Effects menu
    Color, Brightness and Contrast, 147
    Sharpen, 146
    Transform roll-up, 25–26
ellipse, placing text on, 50–52
Ellipse tool, 2, 95
    in Corel PHOTO-PAINT, 152
    Ctrl key with, 5
Encapsulated PostScript files, 73
*.eps file format, 72, 123, 132
Eraser tool, in Corel PHOTO-PAINT, 139
Exit (File menu), 17
exiting CorelDRAW, 17
Export (File menu), 72, 74
Export EPS dialog box, 73
Export File dialog box, 72
exporting
    for Corel PHOTO-PAINT, 74–75
    files, 72–73
Eyedropper tool (Corel PHOTO-PAINT), 141, 149

F

file format, exporting to different, 72
file manager. *See* Corel MOSAIC
File menu
    Exit, 17
    Export, 72, 74
    Import, 36, 61, 80, 123
    Mosaic roll-up, 38
    New, 19
    New From Template, 75
    Open, 69, 77
    Print, 16, 71, 125
    recent files listed in, 19
    Save, 9

File menu (Corel MOSAIC)
  New Collection, 107
  Open Collection, 103, 106, 112, 114
  Preferences, 115
  Print Thumbnails, 115
File menu (Corel PHOTO-PAINT), Save
  As, 156
File menu (CorelTRACE), 119, 131
  Save Trace As, 122
files
  attaching keywords to multiple,
    110–112
  exporting, 72–73
  finding with keywords, 112–113
  importing, 80–81
  keyword descriptions, 109–113
  locating in File menu, 19
  printing to, 71–72
fill
  default settings for, 85–86
  for objects, 22
Fill Color tool, 85
Fill flyout, 35, 49, 60
Fill roll-up, 50
  in Corel PHOTO-PAINT, 152
Fill tool, 2, 85
  in Corel PHOTO-PAINT, 153
filters, applying to entire image, 145–146
finding files, with keywords, 112–113
Fit Text To Path (Text menu), 51–52, 95–96
Fit Text To Path roll-up, 51–52
Flatten control, for brush height, 139
flyout menus, 10
fonts
  changing, 55
  selecting in Corel PHOTO-PAINT, 154
Fountain Fill dialog box, 21
Fountain Fill tool, 21
Fountain fills, 50
Fountain Steps print option, 71
Freehand tool, 2, 14, 23, 45, 53
  vs. Bezier tool, 20
Full-Color Pattern fills, 50

Full justification of text, 63
Full-Screen Preview button (ribbon bar),
  93–94

G

grid, 98–99
Grid & Scale Setup (Layout menu), 98
Group (Arrange menu), 100
groups of objects, 25–28
guidelines, 86–87
  deleting, 92–93
  moving, 91
  to position clip art and symbols, 90
Guidelines Setup (Layout menu), 86, 91,
  92–93

H

half-circles, 6
Header dialog box, for printing thumbnails, 116
height for printing, 70
Horizontal Guidelines, 86
Horizontal Mirror button (Transform
  roll-up), 26, 92

I

Image Header (Export EPS dialog box), 73
Import (File menu), 36, 61, 80, 123
Import button (ribbon bar), 88
Import dialog box, 37, 80, 123
Import Files dialog box, 61
imported pictures, changing size, 89
importing
  clip art, 36–38, 88–90
  files, 80–81
  text, 61–62
  traced image into CorelDRAW, 122–124
Include Header (Export EPS dialog box), 73
installing CorelDRAW, and symbols availability, 87

K

Keyword Search dialog box, 113
keywords
    in Corel MOSAIC, 109–113
    finding files with, 112–113
Keywords dialog box, 110

L

Landscape orientation, 83
launching CorelDRAW, 1
    by double-clicking Corel MOSAIC
        thumbnail, 105
Layout menu
    Grid & Scale Setup, 98
    Guidelines Setup, 86, 91, 92–93
    Page Setup, 83
lightening images, 145
Line Precision drop-down list (Tracing Op-
    tions dialog box), 134
Line tool, 155
Linear fountain fill, 21–22
lines
    drawing, 14–16
    placing text on, 53–54
    straight, 15
List Files Of Type drop-down list, in Corel
    MOSAIC, 104, 106
Local Undo tool, in Corel PHOTO-
    PAINT, 139, 150–151

M

Magic Wand (+) tool, 127, 128
magnifying. *See also* Zoom tool,
        zooming in.
    text, 58
magnifying glass icon, 30
Maintain Aspect option, for printing, 70
margins, for paragraph text, 64
marquee selection box, 27, 58, 128
Mask Picker tool, 147
menus, 82

flyout, 10
Minimize button (Mosaic roll-up), 39
Minimize button (Text roll-up), 14
minimizing CorelTRACE, 122
Mirror button (Transform roll-up), 26, 92
mirroring objects, 26
moving
    guidelines, 91
    objects, 24
    roll-up windows, 54
    Toolbox, 18–19, 148
multiple images, tracing, 131–132
multiple objects
    changing text attributes, 65–67
    selecting, 25, 54

N

New (File menu), 19
New Collection (File menu), 107
New From Template (File menu), 75
New From Template dialog box, 75
newsletter, template for, 76
No Outline tool, 10
nodes, 7, 24
    of letters, 59
Normal view, 97
    in Corel PHOTO-PAINT, 141
number of symbol, 40, 88

O

objects
    arranging, 41–44
    blending, 149–150
    changing order, 44
    clicking on selected, 7
    closing, 22
    copying, 79–80
    creating in Corel PHOTO-PAINT,
        151–154
    deleting, 23
    filling, 22
    grid to line up, 98–99

moving, 24
outlines of, 9–11
removing outlines, 10
rotating, 7
selecting multiple, 25, 54
stretching and mirroring, 26
Open (File menu), 69, 77, 119, 131
Open Collection (File menu), 103, 106, 112, 114
Open Collection dialog box, 112
Open dialog box (CorelTRACE), 119
Open Drawing dialog box, 69, 77
order of objects, changing, 44
Outline (Trace menu), 121, 128, 131, 134
Outline Dialog tool, 11, 15, 46, 84
Outline menu, 10
Outline Pen dialog box, 11, 15–16, 46, 85
Outline tool, 2, 9–11, 15, 46, 84
outlines
changing, 45–46
default settings, 84–85
of objects, 9–11
for text, 31

P

Page Setup (Layout menu), 83
page view, 32
paint color, in Corel PHOTO-PAINT, 136
paper color, in Corel PHOTO-PAINT, 136
Paper Color color palette, 84
paragraph text, 61–65
copying, 78–79
entering, 64–65
full justification, 63
margins for, 64
modifying, 63–64
Paragraph Text tool, 65
Paste (Edit menu), 27, 79
path
for imported text file, 62

placing text on, 94–95
*.pcx file format
for Corel PHOTO-PAINT, 74
importing, 80
tracing, 119
Pen tool, 142, 155
photo touch-up, 136–158
Pick tool, 2, 3, 4, 10, 24
marquee selection box from, 27
to select image portion for tracing, 130–131
pie wedges, 6–9
pixels, smoothing, 134
point size of text, 12, 154
Preferences (File menu), 115
preview, 94
of image filter, 146
Preview Image, before printing, 70
Print (File menu), 16, 71, 125
Print dialog box, 16, 70, 125
Print File Name option, for thumbnails, 116
Print Options dialog box, 116
printing, 16
in Corel PHOTO-PAINT, 156–157
to file, 71–72
options, 69–71
Preview Image before, 70
thumbnails, 114–117
traced image, 125–126
problem solving, viewing text in frame, 62
program icon, in Corel MOSAIC, 104

Q

quarter-circles, 8

R

Rectangle Mask tool, 147
Rectangle tool, 2, 29, 31, 49
in Corel PHOTO-PAINT, 152

Ctrl key with, 5

rectangles, 2–5
placement behind text, 60
rounding, 28–29
selecting, 3
textured fill for, 35

Repeat (Edit menu), 100

Repeat Duplicate (Edit menu), 25

resolution, for exporting file, 74

Restore To Checkpoint command, 151, 153

retouch tools, 144–147

ribbon bar, 2, 82–83
Align button, 100
in Corel PHOTO-PAINT, 136, 154
Full-Screen Preview button, 93–94
Wireframe button, 93

roll-up windows, 13. *See also specific types*
moving, 54

Rotate control, for brush angle, 139

rotating
clip art, 39
text, 46–47

rotating and skewing highlighting box, 7
for text, 47

rounding rectangles, 28–29

rulers, 18

S

Save (File menu), 9

Save Drawing dialog box, 9, 77

Save Options dialog box, for tracing, 120

Save Trace As dialog box, 122

saving
Corel PHOTO-PAINT image, 156
drawing, 9
traced image, 122

Scale option, for printing, 71

scanned images
retouching, 136
tracing, 118

scrolling color palette, 28

searching clip art directories, 113

selected objects, clicking on, 7

selected text, changing characteristics, 55

selecting
circles, 6
column of text, 76–77
multiple objects, 25, 54
multiple text objects, 67
rectangle, 3
text, 12, 47, 51

service bureau, printing file at, 72

Shape tool, 2, 6, 7, 8, 24, 29, 59

Sharpen tool, 144–145

Shift key, to select multiple objects, 25

Show Grid option, 98

Show Guidelines option, 86–87

Show list box (Uniform Fill dialog box), 86

silhouette method of tracing, 128–129

size
of page, 83
of printed thumbnail, 115

sizing
symbols, 40
text, 12, 31, 47, 56, 58

sizing handles, 3, 4, 89
for clip art, 37
for symbols, 41

Smear tool, 144

Smooth Dithering, as tracing option, 134

Smudge tool, 149

Snap To Grid, 98–99

Snap To Guidelines, 86
vs. Snap To Grid, 99

Special menu, Symbols roll-up, 40

speed
of printing, 71
of tracing, 121
wireframe view and, 93

Spraycan tool, 143, 149

spraying, color, 142–143

squares, creating, 5

starting CorelDRAW, 1

by double-clicking Corel MOSAIC thumbnail, 105
starting Corel MOSAIC, 102
status line, in application window, 19
straight lines, 15
stretching
    objects, 26
    text, 51
Style box (Outline Pen dialog box), 16
Styles, in Texture Library drop-down list, 35
styles of fonts, changing, 55, 97
symbols, 39–41, 87–88
    breaking into separate parts, 42
    on CD-ROM, 36, 37
    color of, 41
    number identification, 40, 88
Symbols roll-up, 40, 87
    Special menu, 40

T

Target Curve Length drop-down list (Tracing Options dialog box), 134
templates, 75–77
text, 44–47, 49–68
    adding and modifying, 11–14, 94–95
    aligning with drawing, 99–100
    background for, 45, 49–50
    character nodes, 59
    color of, 12, 31, 47, 97
    copying attributes, 96–97
    in Corel PHOTO-PAINT, 154–155
    curving, 50–53
    editing, 56–61
    importing, 61–62
    magnifying, 58
    modifying characteristics, 57, 65–67
    modifying individual letters, 58–59
    outline for, 9–11, 31
    paragraph, 61–65
    placement on path, 53–54, 94–95
    rectangle placement behind, 60
    rotating, 46–47

selecting, 12, 47, 51
selecting multiple objects, 67
sizing, 12, 31, 47, 56, 58
stretching, 51
Text menu
    Edit Text, 56
    Fit Text To Path, 51–52, 95–96
    Text roll-up, 12–13
Text roll-up, 12–13, 55, 96
    Center Justification, 13, 56
    Minimize button, 14
Text tool, 30
    in Corel PHOTO-PAINT, 154
    to open flyout menu, 14
Texture Fill dialog box, 35, 50
Texture Fill tool, 35, 49, 60
Texture fills, 50
Texture Library drop-down list, 60
    Styles, 50
thumbnails in Corel MOSAIC, 38–39, 103–106
    double-clicking to start CorelDRAW, 105
    printing, 114–117
*.TIF file format, 136
Tile Horizontally (Window menu), 108
Tile Vertically (Window menu), 108
Tool Settings roll-up, 139, 142
    for Blend tool, 144
    for Line tool, 155
    for Sharpen tool, 145
    for Smudge tool, 150
Toolbox, 18
    in Corel PHOTO-PAINT, 136
    moving and reshaping, 30, 148
tools, displaying, 19
Trace menu
    Edit Options, 134
    Outline, 121, 128, 131, 134
    Silhouette, 129, 130
    Woodcut, 121
tracing, 119–121

editing image in Corel PHOTO-
PAINT, 126–127
modifying image after, 122–125
multiple images, 131–132
part of image, 127–128
printing image after, 125–126
saving image after, 122
setting options, 133–135
silhouette method, 128–129
speed of, 121
Tracing Options dialog box, 134
Transform roll-up, 25–26, 92
Mirror button, 92
stretch and mirror, 26
Two-Color fills, 50
typeface. *See* fonts

U

Undo (Corel PHOTO-PAINT), 150–151
Undo (Edit menu), 23, 121
Undo Fill (Edit menu), 5
Ungroup (Arrange menu), 124
Uniform Fill dialog box, 84, 85
Uniform fills, 50

V

view
changing, 93
normal, 97, 141
page, 32
preview, 70, 94, 146
View menu
Fill roll-up, 152

Rulers, 18
Toolbox, Floating, 18
viewing text in frame, 62

W

white, setting uniform fill to, 86
width
of outline, 46
for printing, 70
window. *See* application window
Window menu
Tile Horizontally, 108
Tile Vertically, 108
Windows Paintbrush, 75
Wingdings (Symbols drop-down list), 40
Wireframe button (ribbon bar), 93
With Extension option, for thumbnail
printing, 116
Woodcut (Trace menu), 121
WordPerfect, exporting graphics for, 73

Z

Zoom In tool, 30, 58
Zoom To Page tool, 32, 44, 59
Zoom To Selected tool, 31–32, 43
Zoom tool, 2
to open flyout menu, 14
zooming in
in Corel PHOTO-PAINT, 140–141
in CorelDRAW, 29–32

Corel PHOTO-PAINT Toolbox

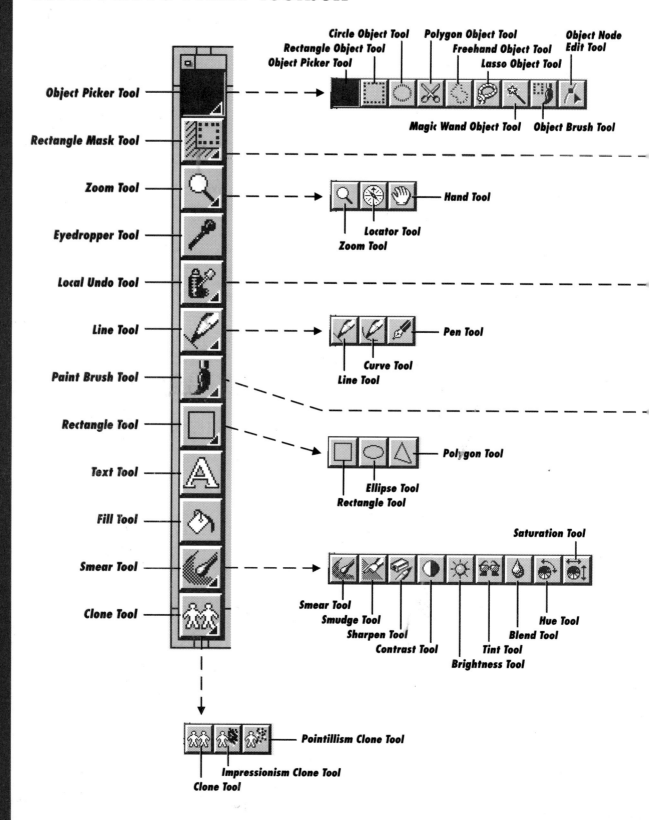

Object Picker Tool

Rectangle Mask Tool

Zoom Tool

Eyedropper Tool

Local Undo Tool

Line Tool

Paint Brush Tool

Rectangle Tool

Text Tool

Fill Tool

Smear Tool

Clone Tool

Object Picker Tool
Rectangle Object Tool
Circle Object Tool
Polygon Object Tool
Freehand Object Tool
Lasso Object Tool
Object Node Edit Tool
Magic Wand Object Tool
Object Brush Tool

Zoom Tool
Locator Tool
Hand Tool

Line Tool
Curve Tool
Pen Tool

Rectangle Tool
Ellipse Tool
Polygon Tool

Smear Tool
Smudge Tool
Sharpen Tool
Contrast Tool
Brightness Tool
Tint Tool
Blend Tool
Hue Tool
Saturation Tool

Clone Tool
Impressionism Clone Tool
Pointillism Clone Tool